Praise for the first edition of
Addictions Counseling:

"Dr. Pita crams an amazing amount of information to produce a counselor's handbook that is both readable and comprehensive. Significantly, the recovery methods of AA and rational emotive therapy are shown to be complementary, an approach the author has used successfully in her own practice. This book is another worthy addition to Crossroad's superb counseling series. Recommended." – *Bookviews*

"A fresh and greatly needed approach to helping the whole person; it fills a great gap in the existing literature."
– Thomas Perrin, author of *I Am an Adult Who Grew Up in an Alcoholic Family*

"A valuable addition to the field." – *Perspectives on Addictions Nursing*

"Valuable. Would serve as a good academic text for chemical dependency counseling programs as well as being a nice addition to any counselor's personal library. It deserves a high rating."
– *Journal of Psychoactive Drugs*

"Counselors just beginning their careers or those who often must do the work of counseling — such as ministers, teachers, and nurses — will greatly appreciate the value of this book as an introduction to the field. Experienced therapists will value the creative insights of the author and her skilled blending of approaches that many have considered antagonistic, such as the two views proposed by Alcoholics Anonymous and cognitive therapy. It is a wise, flexible, and openminded guide that pulls together the contemporary knowledge about substance abuse into one source."
– Dr. William van Ornum

ADDICTIONS COUNSELING

ADDICTIONS
COUNSELING

A PRACTICAL AND COMPREHENSIVE
GUIDE TO COUNSELING PEOPLE
WITH ADDICTIONS

REVISED AND UPDATED EDITION

DIANNE DOYLE PITA

A Crossroad Book
The Crossroad Publishing Company
New York

The Crossroad Publishing Company
www.CrossroadPublishing.com

Printed in the United States of America

The text is set in 10/13 Garamond Antiqua.

Library of Congress Cataloging-in-Publication Data
Pita, Dianne Doyle.
    Addictions counseling : a practical and comprehensive guide to counseling people with addictions / Dianne Doyle Pita. – Rev. and updated.
        p. ; cm.
    Includes bibliographical references.
    ISBN 0-8245-2262-1 (alk. paper)
    1. Substance abuse – Patients – Counseling of. 2. Substance abuse – Patients – Rehabilitation. 3. Substance abuse – Treatment.
    [DNLM: 1. Substance-Related Disorders – therapy. 2. Counseling – methods.
WM 270 P681a 2004] I. Title.
RC564.P58 2004
616.86′06 – dc22

                                                                2004002424

Contents

ACKNOWLEDGMENTS

I dedicate this book to all those people with addictions trying to defeat the enemy of addiction and all those counselors on the front line fighting alongside of them. To all those still out there losing the battle, I hope that we can find a way to reach you, soon. To the millions who have passed on having lost the battle with addictions, addictions that robbed them of their will to see the beauty of reality and convinced them that living a life sober is not living at all, I hope that we have learned from them and that knowledge is used to better help others live a life free of the haze of addiction.

INTRODUCTION

Twelve years have passed since my writing of the first edition of *Addictions Counseling*. Since then I have taught and supervised hundreds of students and treated many patients. My enthusiasm has not dwindled over the years; if anything I am more committed to helping people recover. There have been developments but no revolutions in the field; we are plugging along using tried-and-true techniques. The field is becoming more professional as more people seek credentials for addictions counseling. There are more counselors and psychotherapists entering the field who are not "in recovery." The need to be treated by someone suffering from the same illness as oneself is now more often seen as a symptom of the disease than anything else. Are we making progress as a society in decreasing the use and abuse of substances? Anecdotal evidence and statistics do not suggest we have won the war against drugs, but we appear to be making some headway. I think more than ever kids are searching for something to fill the void in their lives, and this leads them to use drugs. We have younger and more emotionally disturbed substance abusers to start with, but we may be improving in positive treatment outcomes. We clearly need to focus efforts on prevention and intervention, and I think that lies in family work.

My life continues to be affected by the disease of addiction, with loved ones passing on and others giving up the fight. This has renewed my commitment to trying to find something that works better. Is there anything new that will help us increase our effectiveness as addictions counselors? Yes, that is what motivated me to write this newly revised and updated edition. In the first edition I presented an integrated approach to addictions counseling, integrating cognitive-behavioral and Twelve Step approaches. I have since discovered the

9

terrific technique of motivational interviewing, developed by Miller and Rollnick. Now I present an integration of cognitive-behavioral and Twelve Step approaches with the motivational approach added. If you can learn and utilize this approach you will increase the effectiveness of your counseling, and you will experience less professional burnout.

A second change in the field is increased recognition of the problem of drugs other than alcohol. I am getting more and more patients with addiction to drugs such as cocaine, marijuana, and heroin. The National Institute of Drug Abuse (NIDA) has given priority to addiction to drugs other than alcohol. In particular, cocaine is a drug of focus today, though heroin is equally a problem. Addiction is considered a brain disease and as such this has opened the way for treatment through medications. There are medications to reduce cravings and medications being developed to reduce damage already done by drug use. I have updated many sections by including the most current research.

A third change is the increased awareness of co-occurring substance dependence and psychiatric disorders. We can expect 30–50 percent of those being treated for substance abuse to also have a psychiatric diagnosis such as depressive or bipolar disorder. I have included information on dual disorders that will provide guidance on how to best treat people with psychiatric disorder who also have a substance abuse problem. Related to both prescription medication (for addiction and for psychiatric disorders) and increasing secondary diagnoses is the ever-rising problem of prescription drug abuse. We are witnessing an increasing use of psychiatric diagnosis and consequent increase in availability of prescription drugs. The negative consequence is a rise in abuse of prescription drugs and the illicit sale of such drugs. In particular, many women I see are routinely prescribed addictive psychiatric medications, and many adolescents are getting drugs from classmates who are selling or abusing their own drugs. Abuse of pain medications is rampant among adults, as is abuse of the overly prescribed medication for attention deficit/hyperactivity disorder (ADHD), particularly popular among adolescents. Women and children are especially vulnerable to prescription drug abuse, and I have included some specific information unique to these two populations.

Some material remains essentially the same, for instance, the discussion of stages of recovery. What else hasn't changed? While awareness of addiction has increased, I do not think we have made significant progress in our attitude toward those with addictions. Some of those in the medical field still lag, at least in my area of the country. There are instances of patients being treated more as criminals needing punishment than as patients with a disease. Being in recovery does not automatically make counselors or others in the "helping" professions empathic or compassionate. Program managers and counselors who are themselves in recovery are often the least aware of their own transference issues and the most punishing of all "helpers." There continue to be far too many instances of treatment programs hiring patients straight out of treatment, too many instances of counselors getting high on the job and not being confronted or being confronted and allowed to return after only a few days to "get their act together." Prejudice toward persons with addictions is like any other prejudice; the anger and disrespect shown toward people with addictions has to do with a lack of education and lack of insight into one's own unresolved issues. The good news is that progress toward professionalism, though slow, is happening. Hope for improved treatment lies in addictions counselors who have empathy, ethics, insight, and motivation.

My students in addictions counseling are terrific, as they have been for the past eighteen years. They have given me positive feedback and motivation to continue to work in the field. I am grateful for their support. Generally, they find my work interesting and easily applied to their work. I find that they will not read a book that is too dry or "textbook-like." Therefore, I have attempted again in this edition to translate the more technical psychojargon into something understandable and useful. It's a tough, frustrating field, with the source of frustration continuing to be more the administration of the programs than the patients themselves. As counselors we continue to be underpaid and underappreciated by our employers. When can we expect equitable pay? There is no way of answering that question. I continue to encourage my students to gain further education and credentials, which ultimately will result in higher pay. But the field continues to hold its greatest rewards for those whose hearts are in helping people recover from addictions. The greatest rewards come from seeing people who once had nothing — no hope, no self-esteem or self-respect, no clothes, job, or housing — find all they need in recovery. Hopefully, this material will further motivate you and make your job easier. Who knows? Maybe when another decade has passed I will be able to write that addictions counselors are now receiving the recognition they deserve.

THE COUNSELOR'S ROLE
IN RECOVERY

Most clinicians and researchers alike believe the counselor-client relationship to be the most important ingredient in effective counseling. Cognitive theorist and practitioner Beck writes, "A collaborative relationship between the therapist and the patient is a vital component of any successful therapy" (Beck et al., 1993). Miller and Rollnick (2002), who developed motivational interviewing, say, "The therapeutic relationship tends to stabilize relatively quickly, and the nature of the client-counselor relationship in early sessions predicts treatment retention and outcome." K. T. Mueser, arguably the best-known clinical researcher in the dual disorder field, states, "The clinician cannot help the patient modify his or her substance use behavior without a therapeutic relationship" (Mueser, Drake, and Noordsy, 1998). Given that the therapeutic alliance is essential to change, we will spend some time examining how a counselor develops this alliance.

In answering the question of how addictions counselors help clients get sober, we begin by asking how the counseling relationship differs from any other helping relationship. Each semester I ask my students to differentiate the various roles in recovery: counselor, sponsor, friend. This task is not easy because most of the students play all three roles, and the boundaries among them blur. For our own survival, we need to recognize the difference between being a friend, a sponsor, and a counselor.

A friendship is *a mutual* relationship. The word "mutual" implies an equal exchange of self and support. The sponsor-sponsoree and counselor-client relationships are not mutual. Sponsors and, especially, counselors do not ask their clients for help in solving their life problems. The sponsor has learned how not to drink or use drugs and, thus, can share this experience with his sponsoree. In sponsoring, there is no assumption of a level of education, training, professional ethics, or emotional well-being. The counselor, on the other hand, is perceived as possessing all of these qualities, and more.

The counseling relationship is unique. It is initiated and continues because the client feels a need for special help with a problem that she is not able to resolve on her own or through other relationships. The counseling relationship is structured in time and space. The relationship does not extend beyond the professional relationship or beyond the four walls of the office. The relationship is limited by time. The client typically sees the counselor once a week and does not have unlimited access to her through phone calls or social visits. The relationship is, however, closer and deeper than ordinary social friendships. Professional ethics and laws of confidentiality apply to this relationship.

Perhaps most important is that the counselor is there solely for the good of the client. The counselor's purpose for that hour-long session is to focus on the client and help the client get better. The counselor is being paid to do that; the client has no obligation, no responsibility for the emotional well-being of the counselor. Because the client does not owe the counselor anything (other than the fee), the client trusts that she has an objective listener. The counselor has no ulterior motive. Often, this is the only relationship the client has in which she does not place the other person's needs before her own. In the process of placing herself first and focusing on her own feelings and needs, the client gains a different perspective on herself in relation to another.

Counselor Qualities

There is surprisingly little dissension in the counseling field in defining the necessary counselor attributes. Even where two counseling approaches are diametrically opposed, they tend to agree on the qualities required of the counselor. There may be disagreement on whether the qualities are "necessary and sufficient" for change or whether they are necessary *but not* sufficient for change. The qualities themselves are, however, basically the same whether we are asking a behaviorist, a psychoanalyst, or a cognitive therapist.

Carl Rogers, who developed self theory and the client-centered approach, has contributed a great deal to our knowledge of what he calls the "necessary and sufficient" conditions for therapeutic personality change. He points out that significant change does not occur except in a relationship. The necessary and sufficient conditions include psychological contact, counselor congruence, counselor empathic understanding, and counselor unconditional positive regard. Congruence refers to the counselor's being genuine or real. Not only does the counselor mean what she says but her feelings also match what she is saying. Empathy involves seeing things through the client's eyes and being able to communicate this experience to the client so that the client knows the counselor understands her. A positive, accepting attitude on the part of the counselor means that she cares about the client as a person with potential. The counselor respects the client as an individual and is nonjudgmental.

One of the most valuable aspects of Rogers's work is that his theory has generated a great deal of research. Research findings support what we would expect to be true: an individual who can communicate warmth, genuineness, and accurate empathy is more effective in helping other people (Truax and Carkhuff, 1967). Based on his research, Carkhuff extended Rogers's theory into an eclectic approach to counseling. The term "eclectic" means an approach that is not tied to a single theory but rather combines selected aspects of various theories. In addition to the core conditions of empathy, positive regard, and genuineness, Carkhuff added concreteness, immediacy, and confrontation. Concreteness involves focusing the client's attention on specific behaviors as they are occurring in the relationship. Immediacy involves the counselor's communicating to the client what the counselor believes the client's behavior means (interpretation). Confrontation means presenting the client with her own behavior by pointing out a discrepancy in that behavior.

These counselor qualities were identified long ago but hold true today. Counselor qualities such as empathy continue to be shown through research to be essential for change. Empathy involves being able to get in the shoes of the client, see things as she sees them, and communicate that understanding to the client. Empathy is not sympathy, which is feeling sorry for someone. Empathy is not identification, which is having in common the past experience. For instance, identification may occur when both the client and the counselor are heroin addicts now in recovery. While having this shared experience may initially facilitate alliance, it may be more difficult for the counselor to maintain objectivity, to not identify with the client. If the counselor identifies with the client rather than demonstrating empathy, she may find herself stuck in the shoes of the client and unable to help either the client or herself. With regard to the expression of empathy, Miller and Rollnick (2002) write, "In fact, a recent personal history of the same problem area (e.g., alcoholism) may compromise a counselor's ability to provide critical conditions of change because of overidentification." The counselor does not impose his own material in expressing empathy. These authors review recent research that shows empathy can determine the clients' response to treatment. For instance, in one study (Miller et al., 1993), they found that drinking outcomes could be predicted from the degree of empathy shown by counselors during treatment. In other words, the more empathic the counselor, the more likely the client was to abstain from alcohol. In contrast, confrontational counseling was associated with a high dropout rate and poor outcomes. The more the counselor confronted the client during treatment, the more the client drank. For counselors still dependent on a "confrontation-of-denial" approach, these findings offer more reasons to develop the technique of empathy.

In *The Helping Interview* (1974), Alfred Benjamin provides added insight into this concept of unconditional positive regard: "We can best help him through behavior that demonstrates that we consider him responsible for himself, his actions, thoughts, and feelings, and that we believe in his capacity to use his own resources increasingly." No matter what the approach, all theorists stress the need for the client to feel that the counselor is concerned and able to help.

The Role of the Counselor in the Counseling Process

Part of our role as helpers, then, involves establishing a trusting and open relationship with the client. Whereas counselor qualities are pretty much the same across approaches, the role of the counselor in the counseling process is very different. The psychoanalysts, and ego-analysts, the rational therapists (rational-emotive therapists such as Ellis, reality therapists such as Glasser), and the learning theorists and behavioral counselors believe that the counselor is some kind of expert to whom the client has come with a problem that she cannot resolve alone. This assumption leads to the belief that the counselor must take a more active or authoritative role in the counseling relationship. They see the counselor as being responsible for making a diagnosis of the problem and for presenting a treatment plan.

At the other end of the continuum of counseling approaches, Rogerians, Gestaltists, and Adlerians argue that because of people's inherent growth tendency or tendency toward self-actualization, the client has the capacity and the motivation to solve his own problem if provided with an accepting positive counseling relationship. Rogers, in advocating his client-centered approach, stresses that the counselor's presence or behavior in the counseling relationship does not directly influence the client's behavior. In the client-centered approach, it is considered very important that the client set the goals. Thus, the role of the counselor is to provide the conditions (e.g., unconditional positive regard); the client will then change on his own within those conditions. Rogers believes that diagnosing the problem and setting treatment goals create dependence needs in the client.

Rogers with his client-centered approach and Ellis with his rational-emotive therapy obviously disagree on the role of the counselor in the relationship. As Ellis states, "The rational therapist does not delude himself that these relationship-building and expressive-emotive methods are likely to really get to the core of the client's illogical thinking" (Ellis, 1962). Relationship techniques are viewed simply as preliminary techniques and, "the rational therapist goes beyond the point to make a forthright, unequivocal attack on the client's general and specific irrational ideas and to try to induce him to adapt more rational ones in their place" (Ellis, 1972). Ellis places responsibility on the client; he views the client as having the capacity to change.

The Counselor's Role in Recovery Counseling

Interestingly, a major point of departure between these approaches is the question of dependence. Ellis, through a didactic or teaching approach, clearly defined treatment objectives, and homework, puts the responsibility on the client. Rogers, on the other hand, believes that client independence and responsibility can be achieved only by setting up the proper external conditions (empathy, positive regard) and then waiting for the client to change. The counseling approach of choice in addictions or recovery counseling would include both components as necessary and sufficient conditions. Recovery from addiction requires counselor qualities and the establishment of a therapeutic relationship as well as clear education, instruction, and a plan of action.

If a client suffering from an addiction comes to us and asks for our expert help in solving his life problems, just on ethical grounds alone, it seems, we need to provide him with an accurate assessment and treatment plan. As addictions counselors, we believe that while the individual is actively engaged in his chemical addiction, he has very little freedom of choice; that is what concepts such as "denial," "loss of control," and "disease" are about. If a cocaine addict comes to us for help and we do not confront him on his addiction problem, it doesn't matter how accepting and genuine we are; he is probably not going to conclude on his own that he must abstain from all drugs.

A major difference in treating the addictions is thus the necessary condition of an active, direct, didactic approach with a clear plan of action. This approach is necessary in the early stages of counseling: assessing the problem, helping the client see that the chemical is the problem, and helping him to stop using the substance. The approaches of Ellis and Rogers, although at the extremes, are not mutually exclusive. We need to understand that confrontation is a part of being genuine and honest. Understanding the complementarity of seemingly opposing concepts is the key to effective addictions treatment. The complementarity of concepts such as "tough love," "responsibility and freedom," and "gaining control by letting go," are basic to understanding the recovery process. We give the clients the tools of sobriety and then we let go, encouraging them to use the tools in their own way.

As addictions counselors, we must be very clear in understanding the difference between accepting a person and accepting a behavior. This is essential to addictions counseling to ensure not only that we accept the client and treat the client effectively but also that we can teach the client to accept himself. We do not accept or pretend to accept the addict's bad (hurtful, self-destructive) behavior. The person, however, we accept as a human being worthy of help. We care about and respect the addicted individual enough to trust that, with psychoeducation and challenges to his unhealthy belief systems within the context of a trusting therapeutic relationship, he can become responsible for making his life what it can be. Later on in recovery, as the client moves out of denial and into a more self-exploratory phase, the conditions outlined by Carkhuff in his eclectic approach, or any other recognized approach for that matter, may prove necessary *and* sufficient in facilitating change.

In addition to bringing ourselves as human beings to the counseling relationship, what else is necessary for change? We must bring our expertise in treating addictions (a knowledge base and experience), we must bring our professional ethics, and we must bring our knowledge and skills in the techniques of counseling. The great distance between knowing how to get a person sober and getting the person to "hear" what we know when we speak is closed by relationship attitudes and skills.

= T W O =

CHOOSING A MODEL
OF ADDICTION

Historically, the scientific community and laypersons have defined alcohol and drug-related problems in their own way, depending on the political and social times and their own personal feelings. How we conceptualize the disease influences how the disease is treated. When society viewed the alcoholic as morally weak, he was ostracized to skid row. Later, the alcoholic was thought to have a physical sickness, a disease, and was treated by physicians in a hospital setting. Today, alcohol and drug addiction is generally defined as a disease by the people treating it; however, there is reluctance on the part of the public and medical professions to recognize it as a *chronic* rather than *acute* disease. The public and professionals alike often think that people should be treated once for this disease, and then they should be able to maintain abstinence on their own.

We are witnessing another shift as insurance companies become unwilling and unable to pay for medical treatment of the chronically relapsing alcoholic and drug addict. Insurance companies are attempting to set a limit on the number of detoxifications a person can have within a period of time. For instance, if a person has five detoxifications in one year and then attempts to go for his sixth within that time period, he may be denied services. The goal is to reduce the detoxification "revolving door" (frequent entrances and exits by the same person). The impact of this change in policy is not yet clear. Will such a policy motivate the addict not to relapse? That is, if the addict knows that he has used up his detoxes for the year, will he think twice about drinking or snorting coke because he doesn't want to end up going through withdrawal on the sidewalk? Or will it simply increase emergency room visits or deaths due to lack of treatment? How we answer that question likely reflects our own beliefs about the cause and maintenance of addictive behavior.

Often in addictions treatment we struggle with the fine line between punishment and allowing the addict to experience the negative consequences of his use. Or between enabling the disease to continue versus appropriate humane response to a suffering person. The way we define and treat the disease of addiction is rarely determined by the scientific community as a response to some scientific truth. The way addiction is defined and treated is often (perhaps always) more a function of what suits society's needs at the time rather than what is best for the patient.

Why is it that our value judgments always enter into our concepts and treatment of addicted individuals? We are caught up in a moralistic debate about the addicted individual. We do not like to see people who lack self-control. What many angry people are saying is: "Why should they get away with their *bad* behavior when I have to be so *good?*" These ill-defined areas of "loss of control" and "willfulness" are ones with which we all struggle. Whether we believe the alcoholic willfully hurt himself and others or we believe that he suffers from a disease over which he has no control ought to be practically irrelevant to us as helpers. Our role is that of helper, not judge and jury. In this way, our position is similar to that of an attorney. A defense attorney does not refuse to represent his client when the client is guilty; that is not an attorney's judgment to make. Must we see every bad behavior as an accident or as an addiction over which the person has no control in order to help the person get better? Bad behavior does not make a bad person. We need to accept the person as a human being who is asking for help, even if he exhibited the bad behavior intentionally. We cannot teach our clients to accept themselves if we do not accept them.

Evolution of Models

Let me briefly describe the evolution of models so that you may begin to develop your own understanding of addiction. There are many models, and I am going to discuss only the major ones. There is the moral model; the medical model including genetic, endocrinological, brain dysfunction, and biochemical theories; the psychological model including psychodynamic learning and personality theories; and the sociological model with its various theories. In the first edition of this book, I wrote only about models of alcoholism. With the upsurge in use of drugs other than alcohol, we need to consider if these models apply as well to other drugs, and indeed most of the models work equally as well for other drugs as for alcohol. All models, however, do not apply equally as well to all drugs. For instance, most people would not say that highly addictive drugs (such as cocaine and heroin) can be used safely in moderation, which is specifically the argument of the temperance model with regard to alcohol.

Moral Model

The moral model was the first model of alcoholism. Moral models emphasize personal choice as a cause of alcohol problems. Within the moral model, alcohol problems are viewed as willful violations of social rules. "The alcoholic is viewed as having a choice of whether to drink or not drink alcohol." As pointed out by Hester and Miller (1989), in their book on alcoholism treatment approaches, this issue of personal responsibility for alcohol problems remains alive and unresolved. As recently as 1988, the U.S. Supreme Court decided that alcoholism was "willful misconduct" and not a "disease" beyond the person's control and responsibility. Again, I think we can see how the basis of this decision had more to do with what is most manageable for society rather than what is optimal for the person with the disease.

Temperance Model

The temperance model was next to arrive on the scene. The temperance movement emphasized the moderate use of alcohol. The cause of alcohol problems was the substance itself. Not until the temperance movement evolved into the Prohibition movement was alcohol banned. People began to rebel as the movement changed from one advocating the moderate use of alcohol to one forcing drinking control through moral and religious pressure. Prohibition did not end the selling and consumption of alcohol; it just pushed it underground in the form of speakeasies, rumrunners, illicit stills, bootleggers, and racketeers. Had the alcohol issue not been used for political gain, Prohibition would probably not have taken place. At any rate, for obvious reasons, the alcohol ban was unpopular and difficult to enforce. In 1933, alcohol again became legal.

Legalizing alcohol created a conceptual dilemma because most Americans believed that alcohol problems were caused by the nature of the substance itself. A solution to this dilemma came in the form of the American disease model of alcoholism. A major assumption of this model is that alcoholism is a progressive condition that is qualitatively different from social drinking. Alcoholics are different from nonalcoholics, causing them to be incapable of drinking in moderation. The central symptom of alcoholism is a loss of control over alcohol, the inability to stop drinking once a person has taken a drink. Although this disease could not be cured, it could be arrested through abstinence.

Moderate drinking was seen as impossible not for everyone, but only for alcoholics. This model was acceptable to social drinkers; they could view drinking as morally right for them, because they were not alcoholics. This model was helpful to alcoholics because it removed the responsibility for the disease and justified humane treatment rather than punishment. The medical profession later accepted the idea of alcoholism as a disease requiring medical treatment.

Characterological Model

Characterological models attribute the causes of alcoholism to personality disturbances. The assumption is that alcoholics are people with certain personality traits (such as oral dependence) and that the resolution of alcoholism requires a restructuring of the personality. The intervention under this model is psychotherapy aimed at resolving unconscious conflicts. In some ways this model overlaps with the Twelve Step programs. Those who believe in the Twelve Step approach assert that recovery involves more than putting down the drink or drug; it involves personality or character change. This belief in the need also to change on the inside is evident in the Fourth Step, which asks the recovering person to take a moral inventory and look at his character defects. A difference between these two conceptions, in practice, is that the focus in A.A. is on stopping the active addiction first and then on internal change. Characterological models often view the addiction only as a symptom. The unwarranted belief is that the symptom will be removed as the person achieves a more mature level of functioning.

Conditioning Model

Conditioning models are based on the belief that problems with drinking are simply learned habits. People learn to drink because either the properties of the alcohol itself are rewarding, e.g., tension reduction and removal of inhibitions, or the behavior of drinking is reinforced, e.g., peer pressure. A number of different treatment strategies rely on classical conditioning (e.g., aversion therapy), in which the drinking of alcohol is punished, or operant learning principles (e.g., community reinforcement approach), in which not drinking is rewarded.

A limitation of this conditioning model is that if it is just a matter of learned behavior then the behavior can be unlearned or relearned. From this conclusion follow attempts to teach the alcoholic to be a social drinker. After all, if it is just a bad habit, then the alcoholic can simply learn to drink more moderately. The problem is that the alcohol has already taken on a significance beyond that found in a social drinker. Were he just a social drinker, the alcohol would not have been worth the losses he has suffered. Logic suggests that the person is taking a risk in attempting to control alcohol intake. Another question raised by such assumptions has to do with drug use. For instance, we may ask: "Can a cocaine addict learn to use cocaine moderately?"

An example of an approach based largely on conditioning principles is the community reinforcement approach (CRA). This approach uses reinforcers, usually available in the community, to help addicted individuals develop a sober way of life. One very effective component of CRA with cocaine addicts is contingency management, which provides vouchers for staying in treatment (Higgens et al., 1994). So, for instance, if your urine toxicology report is negative for illicit drugs then I might reward you with a small amount of money or a coupon that can be exchanged for clothes or a movie rental.

Neurobiology Model

In the first edition of this book, I wrote briefly about the biological models that emerged in the 1970s. These models focus on genetic and physiological processes as causes of addictive behavior. Some have stressed the importance of hereditary risk factors, whereas others suggest that there are unique biological conditions that predispose some individuals to alcohol and drug dependence. A number of studies of twins have shown a hereditary or genetic component to alcoholism (Bohman, 1978; Goodwin, 1976).

A major change since that writing is the increasing recognition of the neurobiological model of addictive behavior. Many scientists today view addictive behavior as a brain disease. The intense desire for the original drug "high" coupled with the wish to avoid the painful physical and affective state of withdrawal drives the persistent need to use drugs despite any and all consequences. In this view addiction is best understood as a brain disease with highly complex and underlying neurobiological mechanisms that are slowly being elucidated through the use of animal models of addiction (e.g., Koob, 2002).

Not only might neurobiology help explain the processes that maintain addiction, it might also help us understand the causes of addiction. For instance, scientists have discovered a mechanism that appears to account for the different levels of euphoria people experience when taking a stimulant drug (NIDA News Release, September 1, 1999). Research results such as these support the theory that brain chemistry may predispose some people to becoming drug abusers.

This model is highly technical, and to understand it presumes a medical background. For our purposes, what is most relevant is the practical applications of this model, and they are significant. For instance, A. I. Leshner (2000) writes that remarkable research and technological advances in the past two decades have proved that brain disruption and damage play central roles in the consequences of drug abuse and addiction. Knowing the nature of a problem, of course, opens the way for systematic attempts to fix it. Thus today finding ways to restore normal brain function after it has been changed by drugs is a main goal of NIDA research. There are two challenges: to reverse the brain changes that underlie addiction, and to reverse the loss of cognitive and motor functions that occurs when drugs damage and kill brain cells.

Treatments that alleviate some drug-related brain damage are already available. Researchers have shown that methadone therapy ameliorates a particular biochemical abnormality in the brains of opiate abusers. The longer patients stayed in therapy, the more this aspect of their brain biochemistry approached normal. Scientists are now developing medications to prevent relapses to cocaine use. An in-depth discussion of the neurobiology of addiction goes beyond the scope of this book; however, references for this model can be found at the online National Institute of Drug Abuse (NIDA) site: www.nida.nih.gov.

Social Learning Model

Proponents of social learning theory believe that addictive behavior is caused (and maintained) by factors such as modeling, expectancies, and lack of coping skills. In modeling, people learn to use and abuse drugs by observing their parents or peers in the community. We know, for example, that children of parents who abuse drugs and smoke cigarettes are more likely to do the same. An intervention is to provide positive models. For teenagers this may be a Big Brother or Big Sister from the community. A sponsor in the Twelve Step program is a role model of sobriety. The role of expectancies in causing and maintaining substance dependence is the most utilized and researched factor in the field of addiction. Expectancies are the expectations or beliefs that people have about what alcohol and other drugs will do for them. Skill training is a major component of addictions counseling. Assertiveness training and anger management are two of the skills most commonly taught. Modeling, expectancies, and skill development all fall under the heading of "cognitive," an approach associated with research clinicians like Aaron Beck and Albert Ellis.

Etiology

As far as the etiology (causes) of alcoholism and addiction to other drugs, factors such as personality traits are not shown to be significant. Many alcoholics or addicts will say, "I have an addictive personality," but this is more likely a consequence than a cause of their addiction. Alcoholics or addicts, studied before they became addicted, were not more likely than the rest of the population to have "addictive personalities." Moreover, people may express addictive personality in different ways — becoming addicted to work, to food, to exercise, to sex, and so forth. So having an "addictive" or "obsessive-compulsive" personality does not necessarily lead to substance dependence. The development of an addiction probably requires several factors, including a genetic or biological one.

While personality traits are not found to cause addiction, there is significant co-occurrence of addiction and mental disorders or personality disorders. For instance, it is estimated that 20 to 50 percent of persons being treated for addictions have a co-occurring psychiatric disorder (Mueser, Drake, and Noordsy, 1998). Do psychiatric disorders cause, or contribute to, the development of addiction or does addiction lead to the development of psychiatric disorders? That is for the clinician to sort out on an individual basis, and strategies for doing so will be discussed later. However, there are gender differences in etiology worth noting at this point. Women tend to have psychiatric problems first followed by substance use disorders; men have the opposite pattern. Women have higher rates of depression, panic disorder, and phobias than male alcoholics. Men with substance disorders are more than twice as likely as women to be diagnosed with conduct disorder and antisocial personality disorders (Brady and Randal, 1999).

Other factors known to cause alcoholism and other addictions include prevalence of addiction in family background and cultural and family patterns around drug use. Etiology (cause) and effect are often confused, as are the significance of etiological and maintenance factors in the treatment of the problem. As counselors we are less concerned with what causes addiction than we are with what maintains the addiction and how we can intervene in this maintenance pattern and prevent further use. Why a person starts using and why a person continues to use, or returns to using, are two separate sets of factors. Once a person has learned how not to drink, why does he return to drinking? Once a person has major negative consequences to her drinking behavior, why does she not stop and stay stopped? A "dry drunk" may not have had specific character traits prior to becoming alcoholic, but he does now, even in the absence of alcohol, because of the emotional and physical damage caused by the drug. Spiritual bankruptcy may not have caused the problem, but it certainly helps maintain the problem.

Which model of addiction is most helpful for the treatment of the person? There are all types of drug users and abusers, but the people we see in treatment programs are not all that varied. They all have problems resulting from their drinking or drugging, and they have not been able to manage these problems on their own. We are not quite sure what the disease model describes or how accurately the description reflects reality. In the earlier A.A. literature, alcoholism was thought to be "like a disease." This view came from the often insidiously progressive course of alcoholism and the frequent failure of willpower alone to ensure successful treatment.

THREE

PHASES AND CATEGORIES OF ADDICTION

There are no absolutes in the addictions field. There is no single pathway of addiction. The phases I present contain symptoms *generally* found within that phase but *not always* found in that phase. For example, the fact that some alcoholics never experience blackouts does not mean that they are not alcoholics. There are various patterns of alcohol and drug dependence, and these patterns change across the life span of an individual depending on internal and external stressors. There are alcohol- and drug-dependent individuals who do get sober on their own. There are others who get sober through self-help groups alone. And then there are the people we see in treatment.

Whereas it is true that some people do not need outside help to get and stay sober and that some people who had problems with alcohol in the past can drink today without obvious problems, those are not the people sitting across from us in our office. If our clients were like those other people, they would not be seeking help with their problem. So even though it is true that not *all* chemical dependencies follow the same phases of progression, those we come across in treatment typically do follow a definite pattern. The people we most often see have the progressive disease of alcoholism, and learning the pathway of that disease helps us to see how far advanced the disease is and helps us to educate the alcoholic as to what he can expect in the future should he continue to drink.

Phases of Addiction

The signs and symptoms of alcohol addiction identified through research (e.g., Jellinek, 1962) can be found in numerous resource books (e.g., Kinney and Leaton, 1983, 2003). This research, which surveyed over two thousand Alcoholics Anonymous members, found a definite pattern to the appearance of symptoms and progression of the disease in terms of increasing dysfunction. The following description of the four phases of chemical addiction are drawn primarily from Kinney and Leaton (1983, 2003).

Prealcoholic Phase

The *prealcoholic phase* is the initial phase, in which the use of alcohol or drugs is socially motivated. The person experiences psychological relief in the drinking situation and seeks out occasions where drinking will occur. A conscious connection is made between alcohol or drugs and psychological relief. Drinking then becomes the means of dealing with stress. Despite these internal markers of alcoholism, the prealcoholic looks no different from the social drinker from the outside. This phase may last from several months to two or more years as the increase in tolerance to the chemical develops. The increase in tolerance is progressively built up to the point that it takes more and more alcohol or other drugs to get the same level of relief. Whereas initially three drinks might give a comfortable feeling of relief, eventually it will take seven or nine.

Prodromal Phase

The *prodromal* (precursory warning) *phase* signals disease onset. A warning signal of this phase is blackouts (alcohol-induced memory loss). Other evidence that alcohol is no longer "just" a beverage but a "need" includes sneaking extra drinks before parties, gulping drinks, and feeling guilty about drinking. Consumption of alcohol is heavy but not necessarily conspicuous, but to look "okay" to the outside world requires effort. The addicted individual begins hiding alcohol or drug consumption, camouflaging heavy drinking or drugging in an effort to avoid facing negative consequences. There is an increased dependence on the chemical with more and more areas of life becoming associated with the use of the chemical.

Crucial Phase

The *crucial phase* includes the key symptom of loss of control. The alcoholic cannot control the amount, yet he can control whether he will take a drink. With loss of control, his drinking is now obviously different from that of the social drinker. This requires explanation so rationalization begins, and at the same time the alcoholic attempts to regain control. Rationalization is a type of denial; the alcoholic comes up with reasons or rational explanations for his drinking and drinking-related behaviors. The alcoholic will attempt to make external changes to control his drinking: periods of abstinence, change in type of alcohol, change in drinking pattern, geographical escape (moves), change of job, and the like. All these attempts are doomed to failure, and the alcoholic responds to this failure by feeling even worse about himself and angry at others.

The alcoholic is now beginning to recognize that there is something wrong, but he does not understand what is happening and begins to feel guilty. Drinking or drugging violates personal values. Blackouts increase as do the problems caused by these blackouts. The alcoholic's inability to stop drinking becomes apparent to an increasing number of other people. There is remorse caused by the inability to stop drinking, but the person does not know what to do about it. There is a great need to prove to others that he is okay. As the person loses control of his life, there are more and more promises to do better. But the promises are broken.

Losses continue to rise in all life areas: personal, social, financial, family, friends, legal. Drinking begins pushing everything else out of the person's life. Life is now alcohol-centered; family life and friendships deteriorate. The alcoholic begins to isolate herself. Nutritional problems begin to develop because of poor eating habits. The first alcohol-related hospitalization is likely.

Chronic Phase

The *chronic phase* begins with drinking starting earlier in the day, and the alcoholic becomes intoxicated almost daily. The person needs a drink or drug to get going in the morning, and oftentimes tremors become noticeable. Alcohol or drugs reduce tremors and help the person to become functional. There is a loss of ordinary willpower. The ability to determine direction and control of life situations decreases. Drinking and drugging take their physical toll. The person feels physically ill most of the time. Health problems become obvious, and organ system disease develops. There is a sudden decrease in alcohol tolerance. Small quantities of alcohol will produce drunkenness. Drug tolerance suddenly increases with larger quantities needed to produce a high. The addicted person no longer gets relief or gets high, but cannot stop and stay stopped. There is moral deterioration, and the alcoholic can no longer maintain her value system. Binges become more common and interfere severely with maintaining a lifestyle. As feelings about self deteriorate, the addicted person always makes sure he is in the company of someone who is worse off than he is. Impaired thinking is evident in memory, problem-solving abilities, and psychomotor skills. Impaired thinking produces high levels of anxiety and panic. The alcoholic can no longer rationalize that his behavior is normal. Defeat is admitted as the person hits bottom.

Categories of Alcoholism

To complicate matters even further, in addition to the different phases of alcoholism, there are also different types or categories of alcoholics (Kinney and Leaton, 1983). The type of alcoholic whose disease is progressive is called a Gamma alcoholic, which is the type just discussed. The Gamma alcoholic undergoes a change in tolerance, withdrawal symptoms, loss of control, and progression from psychological to physical dependence. The Gamma alcoholic is referred to as the American alcoholic because this type is more common in the United States than in other countries.

Other types or categories of alcoholism have been identified. The Alpha alcoholic is psychologically dependent on alcohol with no loss of control. Relief drinking (drinking to cope, or, actually, not cope) leads to problems with family or, actually, work with no progression evident. We may call this type a problem drinker.

Another type of alcoholic found in cultures with widespread drinking and poor diet is the Beta alcoholic. The Beta alcoholic has various physical problems resulting from drinking such as cirrhosis or gastritis, but the individual is not psychologically or physically dependent on alcohol. Delta alcoholism is very similar to Gamma but without loss of control. The drinker can control his intake but cannot stop drinking for even a day without suffering withdrawal symptoms. Finally, there is Epsilon alcoholism, which is periodic alcoholism marked by binge drinking.

Since there are various types of alcoholics, and since some alcoholics do not need continued external help to manage their disease, clients in treatment often argue against a treatment plan that includes objectives such as continued self-help group attendance and total abstinence. I often use the following reasoning in response to such arguments: "You are in treatment so you are already not like those individuals who did not need treatment to stop. You are in America, not in another country, so chances are you are an American, or Gamma, alcoholic. Therefore, you can expect your disease to progress if you do not abstain from alcohol and other drugs."

Several questions routinely arise regarding progression and recovery. "Does the alcoholic or addict have to get to the final phase before she can get sober?" The answer to this question is no. Everyone's bottom is different, and the bottom seems related to the person's value system. Some people will give up alcohol if threatened with the loss of their family; others will do so if they are threatened by loss of their job. Some addicts quit when they see themselves behaving in ways that are so contrary to their values that they can no longer stand it: prostituting themselves, for example.

A related question is always raised: "Does coercion work or does the person have to 'want' to give up the drug?" Coercion does work. Practically all addicted individuals enter treatment because they have been pushed by others to do so. The level of coercion varies, but rarely does the addicted person willingly seek treatment with the goal of not ever having another drug or drink. Coercion works because it clears the mind and body of chemicals, allowing the person to begin to see what he is doing to himself. Often, given that time, the person no longer wants to continue on the self-destructive path. People who entered treatment because they were threatened with a loss of license (e.g., nurses and physicians) or other job loss appear to recover at no slower a rate than those who are not coerced into treatment.

A third common question is: "Is it true a person has to get sober for himself and not for anyone else?" I do not find this to be true. I think we do not really know what the person's motives are for getting sober. Parents of young children often say they got sober only for their children. A mother may say she is getting sober for her children, but that is because she wants what is best for her children. So in that sense it is for her and for the children. Many women will say they are getting sober for someone else, at least initially, simply because they feel they alone are not worth the time and effort.

A final question has to do with the relationship between chemical addiction and other addictions or dependencies such as food, sex, or gambling. Except for the chemically addictive aspect, the process of dependence and recovery appears essentially the same. The primary difference is that with some of these other addictions the goal is not abstinence but moderation, for example, with food and sex. Learning to use moderately as opposed to abstaining makes recovery somewhat different. By means of internal cues the individual must learn to distinguish use from abuse. For instance, a person addicted to food learns to distinguish between a feeling of hunger and a feeling of emotional emptiness. He then learns how to deal with the feeling of emptiness without filling it up by taking in a substance. We must always be aware that there is no known "cure" for addiction. There is no single pathway to addiction or recovery. We need to keep our minds open to possibilities we would otherwise miss.

= F O U R =

COGNITIVE THERAPY

There are many well-known cognitively oriented therapists, including Aaron Beck, Albert Ellis, Charlotte Buhler, George Kelly, Arnold Lazarus, E. Lakin Phillips, and Julian Rotter. From these theorists have emerged probably over one hundred variations of a cognitive approach. But underlying all approaches and variations is simply the belief that our behavior is influenced by our thoughts. We are not upset by events in our life but by our perception of events. Change the thought, change the behavior. Both Ellis and Beck have applied cognitive therapy specifically to addictions and, therefore, I will rely largely on their techniques and strategies for change (Ellis et al., 1988; Beck, 1993).

Albert Ellis's cognitive approach is called rational emotive therapy (RET). RET was originated by Ellis in 1955 and has become one of the most comprehensive, integrative, and popular schools of psychotherapy practiced. Originally a psychoanalyst, Ellis found that he could help clients overcome their disturbances through more direct, time-, and cost-efficient means. Rather than passively listening to their free associations, Ellis began helping clients actively challenge and dispute their dysfunctional and irrational beliefs and to act against them.

RET is a cognitively and behaviorally oriented theory and practice, emphasizing active, direct, and systematic interventions in the here-and-now (the moment or immediate present). Whereas psychodynamic therapists focus primarily on past events and unconscious processes and behavioral counselors focus on environmental contingencies, RET therapists concentrate on people's *current* beliefs, attitudes, and self-statements as contributing to or causing and maintaining their emotional and behavioral disturbances. RET emphasizes "individuals' innate capacities to change their thinking in order to live happy and productive lives" (Ellis et al., 1988).

The primary assumption is that people can change their feelings and behavior by changing their beliefs. According to the ABCD model of RET, negative life events we often confront are called Activating Events, or As, and the emotions and behaviors that subsequently accompany these events are called the Consequences, or Cs. People will claim that negative Activating Events in their lives (or in their pasts) actually cause their current distress. In contrast, RET holds that it is their thoughts and Beliefs, or Bs, about Activating Events that primarily and more directly cause their disturbances. We then teach the client to challenge or Dispute (Ds) the identified faulty belief and change the belief into a valid one. For instance, a client may state: "The reason I drank was because I went to a wedding where everyone else was drinking so I felt I should be able to drink too." The Consequence is that the client drank. The Activating Event that she is blaming for her drinking is everyone else drinking at the wedding. The faulty Belief is that "I too *should* be able to drink." The Dispute of the faulty Belief is "Why *should you* be able to drink? When was the last time you could drink socially and safely?" The client is taught and encouraged to "do ABCDs" on her irrational feelings and behaviors.

Here is another example that provides evidence that the theory is correct. If I surprised my class with a pop quiz, there would be various responses, or Cs. Some students would feel angry, others anxious, and still others happy. They would say they feel this way because of A, the surprise quiz. But, were it simply A, the same event for all students, then the response would be the same. The response is not the same. What causes these various feelings are the students' Bs, or Beliefs, about the surprise quiz. They feel anger if they believe I *should not* give a surprise quiz. They feel anxiety if they believe they will fail or not do as well as they *should*. And, if they do not pass the test or do not get the grade they *must* get, then they feel like failures. These faulty beliefs are the recipe for test anxiety. Feeling happy or excited would result from a belief that the student knows her stuff and has done well in the past on exams. We obviously do not need to dispute functional or valid beliefs.

In addictions counseling, we are working at changing addictive thinking. Addictive thinking refers to the alcoholic or drug-dependent individuals' set of beliefs, self-statements, and attributions about: (a) their problem with alcohol or other drugs, (b) the many disturbed emotions that this problem causes and the disordered emotions produced in their attempts to change, and (c) themselves as people. We teach the client how to dispute her own beliefs. Disputing is the process of challenging the irrational beliefs. For instance, the A.A. slogan "Let go, let God" challenges the irrational belief that we need to be in control of everything. "Progress not perfection" challenges the belief that we must do everything perfectly. We need to show the clients in a direct and personally meaningful way that their thoughts, feelings, and substance abuse behaviors are all connected. The clients are shown that they can stop their destructive behavior by challenging their irrational or faulty beliefs.

Which beliefs we focus on depends on the stage of recovery. Initially, alcoholics or drug addicts will experience emotional distress as a result of their strongly held self-defeating beliefs about their drinking or using or about being labeled an alcoholic or drug addict. Later in counseling, these clients may also experience maladaptive emotions and irrational thoughts about the feelings of discomfort they experience as they make an effort to change. For instance, they may have the belief that they "can't stand feeling this way!" when they choose not to drug or drink. They do discover, however, that they can stand it and, in fact, are tolerating it. Finally, when alcohol- or drug-dependent people have stopped drinking and drugging and have overcome their dysfunctional thoughts related to this change, they can then focus on their faulty beliefs about coping with everyday life, which largely involves accepting the reality that life is a struggle.

Consistent with Ellis, Beck defines cognitive therapy as "a system of psychotherapy that attempts to reduce excessive emotional reactions and self-defeating behavior by modifying the faulty or erroneous thinking and maladaptive beliefs that underlie these reactions." As applied to substance abuse, the cognitive approach helps individuals come to grips with the problems leading to emotional distress and to gain a broader perspective on their reliance on drugs for pleasure or relief from discomfort.

Relapse prevention is a cognitive behavioral technique essential to addiction treatment. Beck, Ellis, Daley, Gorski, and others describe a cognitive model of relapse. These models are essentially the same. Maintaining behavioral change proves to be more difficult than the initial quitting. Most people who quit have a lapse or relapse, most likely within ninety days of beginning abstinence. A lapse or "slip" is defined as the initial use of a substance after a person has made a commitment to abstain. A relapse, in contrast, is defined as a return to maladaptive behaviors originally associated with the use of the substance. There is much disagreement regarding the concepts of "slip" and "relapse." Some do not believe there is a difference between the two, pointing out that people build up to drink (BUD), meaning that relapse is a process that precedes the actual use of a substance. The process preceding use may be referred to an "emotional relapse." Prior to picking up the drug or the drink the client may demonstrate a change in behavior (e.g., missing appointments) or attitude (apathy replacing desire to abstain, increased levels of anger, justifying or romanticizing use), and so forth. The counselor's goal is to recognize the symptoms of relapse as soon as possible in order to intervene with relapse prevention.

According to Beck et al. (1993), the cognitive model of relapse is nearly identical to the model of ongoing use. The cocaine addict, e.g., is vulnerable to high-risk stimuli or triggers that stimulate his appetite for drugs. These stimuli are both internal (depression, loneliness, anger, frustration, physical pain) and external (people, places, and things that are related to use.) Some triggers are common to most addicts, e.g., being in a barroom is an external trigger for many alcoholics. Being Hungry, Angry, Lonely, Tired (HALT) are common internal triggers. Other triggers are individual. For some addicts, having a pocketful of cash is a trigger; for others having no money is a trigger.

The key to cognitive therapy is individualization: we must collect information from the client until we can see things through her eyes. For example, it is not enough information if the client says, "My boyfriend and I had a big blowout last night and I got drunk afterward." What exactly was the argument about? What were the words spoken? What were the thoughts underlying the feelings and behavior? How can we challenge the faulty beliefs to help the client cope with the situation? Triggers activate drug-related faulty beliefs such as: "I can get away with having one drink," "Drugs will cure my depression," "I can't be part of the group without doing drugs," and so forth. These thoughts may trigger automatic thoughts: "I can't stand not having a drink," or "I need a hit!" and these thoughts, in turn, trigger cravings and urges (internal cues). The person may respond to these cravings with drug-seeking behaviors. Once the person has learned alternative coping strategies, she may challenge these faulty beliefs with self-statements such as "I want a drink but I don't need a drink," "If I have a drink I may feel better for the moment but then my life will be as hopeless as ever," "I can't have just one drink." Along with learning these new beliefs to challenge the old, the person needs to learn new behaviors such as calling a friend or going to a meeting. A related goal of relapse prevention is to help the person get back on track if she does relapse. New beliefs are taught to challenge old beliefs that prolong the slip or relapse. For instance, the person may believe that now that she has slipped it's all over, and she might as well go on a binge. A new thought is: "I did have a slip, but I can prevent further damage by stopping now."

FIVE

ETHICS FOR PROFESSIONALS
WORKING WITH ADDICTS

The addictions field, still relatively new, has its own code of ethics, last revised in 1995 by the National Association of Alcohol and Drug Abuse Counselors (NAADAC). In their book on ethics, Bissell and Royce (1987, 1994) cover issues such as confidentiality and mandated reporting, finance and funding, competence, patient rights, exploitation of clients, and professional relations. Another excellent resource for ethical questions is a book by White (2001). This is a hands-on case study guide with approximately two hundred examples of ethical dilemmas. Each case is followed by a list of the major ethical issues at conflict in the scenario. Although these books are directed toward addictions professionals, that is, those whose primary function is that of professionals or therapist, addictions counselors are not the only ones affected by these issues. Many helpers (medical professionals, psychologists, social workers, school guidance counselors, clergy) need to be educated about the disease of addiction and how humanely to manage persons with an addiction.

Impaired Professionals

Impairment refers to objective change in a person's professional functioning. For example, work assignments are incomplete; conflict with colleagues has increased; clients, students, or families have registered complaints; absenteeism and tardiness have increased. Often the deterioration in work behavior is not publicly known. For example, in cases of impairment involving sexual abuse, the impairment becomes known only when complaints by patients are reported to other professionals or to the state's ethics committees. Most fields are now willing to admit that a problem of impaired professionals does exist, and they have developed programs for dealing with the impaired professional. This has occurred in medicine, dentistry, pharmacy, nursing, law, psychology, psychiatry, and the clergy.

When I wrote the first edition of this book over a decade ago, the issue of professional impairment was much more in the closet than it is today. The increased awareness of sexual abuse by helpers is due largely to the massive clergy sexual abuse scandals that we have lived through in recent years. We witnessed the incredible denial not only of the priests who preyed on the children, but also of the church authorities and the parents. Covering up known sexual abuse by priests eventuated in hundreds more children being victimized. Substance abuse on the part of the helper increases the likelihood of abuse; this connection becomes obvious in the cases of sexual abuse by priests when we see how often alcohol and other drugs are involved. As addictions counselors, we cannot put our heads in the sand and pretend that unethical and illegal behavior on the part of counselors does not exist. It does, and far too frequently, and far too frequently there is no negative consequence for the counselor's behavior. We are responsible for the welfare of *the client* first and foremost, not protecting another counselor's reputation or job.

Firsthand descriptions of professional impairment related to chemical dependence, depression, or common life stresses such as divorce or loss of a loved one, chronic illness, and sexual abuse of the client are limited but available. One book with self-report case examples is *Wounded Healers: Mental Health Workers' Experiences of Depression* (Rippere and Williams, 1985), and there is a more recent book available on patients as victims of sexual abuse (Jehu et al., 1995). Three very good books written by clients describing the relationships in depth are also available. Pope and Bouhoutsos (1986) present some common scenarios, and Gonsiorek (1987) and Schoener (1987) describe characteristics of therapists.

What can we do about the type of impairment that leads to the sexual abuse of a patient? Largely, there is little we can do about the abuse of client by a counselor who has rationalized that abuse and finds it acceptable. I do not believe that education is going to stop such counselors and therapists because they believe they are the exception to the rule. For some reason it is okay for them; somehow they are helping, not hurting, the patient. Although a discussion of issues may not prevent the sexual abuse of a patient, we may become more vigilant toward this behavior in our colleagues, and we may be more likely to believe our clients when they report such behavior. Moreover, although this extreme abuse may not be stopped, other more subtle forms of misused power by more benign therapists may be. We can recognize our own vulnerabilities, watch for the red flags, and take steps to keep the client-therapist boundaries in check.

Let us begin to look at the range of impairment. There are gender differences in the reporting of sexual abuse by counselors; males are primarily the perpetrators and females are the victims. I say "reporting" rather than committing the abuse because we really do not know for certain whether males are just less likely than females to report sexual abuse. It is likely, however, that more male therapists sexually abuse their female clients than female therapists abuse their male patients. This is probably a reflection of our society. Women are more often viewed as sexual objects with men being portrayed as dominant and controlling in sexual encounters. Sex is portrayed as a way for men to feel in control and to express their anger at women. Some male therapists even convince themselves that sex with a female client is therapeutic.

I know of many cases in which a female counselor became romantically and sexually involved with a male patient. A gender difference is operating here in that it seems more acceptable (to the counselor and her peers) for a female counselor to become romantically and sexually involved with a male patient than for a male counselor to become involved with a female patient. We are not sufficiently aware, as a society, of the fact that men, too, are emotionally and sexually victimized with the same consequences as those for women.

What is wrong with this behavior? Everything. The counselor-client relationship is not a mutual one. The clients come to the helping professional because they are not coping well with life, they are addicted to something or someone, and they need help breaking away. They view the professional as having the power to "cure" them. They place their faith in the therapist and trust that the therapist will act in their best interest. The therapist is guiding the relationship and is in control of the relationship. The relationship becomes very important to the client. The therapist is supposed to be the healthy one, and the client is supposed to be the sick one. Clients are paying us to use our professional knowledge and techniques to help them get better. To then betray that trust by using the client to satisfy one's own needs is obviously wrong. The patient will never view the sexual or romantic encounter in the same way the therapist does. There is very little difference between this type of sexual abuse and child sexual abuse because of the vulnerability in both cases to adult authority. We cannot allow professional helpers to feed their egos by victimizing their clients and patients.

With regard to "love relationships," which are more common than we might imagine, the same reasoning applies. How can a sick person choose an intimate partner? This phenomenon of the patient's attachment to the helper always reminds me of Dr. Konrad Lorenz's imprinting experiments with geese. The newborn goslings will dutifully follow any object regardless of how inappropriate that object is for their development. The goslings became imprinted or bonded to Dr. Lorenz. How can a counselor choose a sick person as a partner in a love relationship? There is no basis for mutuality, which is the essence of intimacy. If there is no intimacy, then why would the counselor choose the person? Simply stated, the patient will dutifully follow the counselor. The counselor is needed, she is in control, and she does not have to deal with the possibility of real intimacy, at least while the patient is sick.

Why do professional helpers who work with addicted individuals need their own code of ethics? There are unique features of the field of addictions that have to do both with the qualities of the client and the helper. A primary difference is that the field of addictions has, traditionally, attracted helpers who have recovered from the same illness as the one they are treating. And when they are not themselves recovered from an addiction, the helpers tend to be people who are affected by the addictions of significant others. What is unique, then, is the overlap between the helper's own personal issues with those of the client. We must be alert to boundary problems and professional codependence.

Codependence in Professionals

Inappropriate intimate involvement with clients does occur, too often and with too few negative consequences for the counselor. I will include such involvement under the umbrella of professional codependence. Professional codependence, although we do not know how common it is across disciplines, must be quite common in the helping field by virtue of the fact that so many helping professionals grew up with the disease of addiction, either in their family or in themselves.

There are as many definitions of codependence as there are of alcoholism. Codependent personality disorder is a dysfunctional relationship with the self characterized by living through or for another, attempts to control others, blaming others, a sense of victimization, attempts to "fix" others, and intense anxiety with regard to intimacy. It is very common in people raised in dysfunctional families and in the partners and children of alcoholics and addicts. As Engel (1990) writes:

> The irony is that as much as a codependent feels responsibility for others and takes care of others, she believes deep down that other people are responsible for her. She blames others for her unhappiness and problems, and feels that it's other people's fault that she's unhappy. Another irony is that while she feels controlled by people and events, she herself is overly controlling. She is afraid of allowing other people to be who they are and of allowing events to happen naturally. An expert in knowing best how things should turn out and how people should behave, the codependent person tries to control others through threats, coercion, advice giving, helplessness, guilt, manipulation, or domination.

These dysfunctional behaviors fit naturally with counseling. Cermak (1986, 1989) helps to clarify the concept of professional codependence. In his book on diagnosing and treating codependence, he defines codependence as follows: "Co-dependence is a recognizable pattern of personality traits, predictably found within most members of chemically dependent families, which are capable of creating sufficient dysfunction to warrant the diagnosis of Mixed Personality Disorders as outlined in DSM-III." His proposed criteria for the diagnosis of codependent personality disorder can be found in his books. Professional codependence is just the extension of codependence to the helping relationship. Many codependent traits and survival behaviors are also valued clinical skills. Codependents have learned to put their feelings on the back burner; they have learned to stay calm in the midst of another's chaos and confusion. They have learned to ignore themselves and focus on the problems of others. Codependents are natural counselors.

Most addicts, in addition to being chemically dependent, are also codependent. Not only does the counselor struggle with codependence, he is also helping a client who is struggling with his own codependence. The limitation of the codependent counselor is that the counselor has little awareness of self as separate from another and, therefore, has great difficulty setting up boundaries in relationships. The result of not having good boundaries causes the counselor to take on too much responsibility for the client's success in treatment. The counselor begins to work harder than the client because his feeling good about himself is dependent upon the client's doing well.

Codependence in relation to a loved one's active alcohol or drug addiction is often referred to as "enabling." The term "enabler" is used to describe the spouse, parent, child, or friend who encourages the substance abuser in subtle and usually unconscious ways. Ellis et al. (1988) describe three types of enablers. The first is the "joiner," the type who openly supports the person's habit. The second is the "silent sufferer." Silent sufferers do not make any attempts to change the substance abuser; they just take it. They absorb the pain and then collude in a conspiracy to deny the problem and to present an image to the world that all is well. The third type, which is typically descriptive of the professional codependent, is the "messiah."

The messiah states his opposition to the loved one's drinking or drug use and wages an open campaign to try to change him or her. In his attempt to help, the messiah usually intervenes for the addict in a way that prevents the addict from suffering the natural consequences of his loss of control. The messiah "understands" the problems and wants to help make things better, so he rescues the alcoholic or drug addict from the negative consequences of substance abuse.

Recognizing Our Own Codependence

We know we are becoming codependent with our clients or patients when we are working harder than they are at their recovery. This is a big tip-off because it is the *result* of codependence. The counselor becomes overly invested in the client's recovery, and his ego becomes involved. If the client does well, the counselor feels well. If the client does poorly, the counselor feels poorly, depressed, angry, even hurt. The less active the client is in his recovery, the more active is the counselor. The counselor is having feelings *for* the client, and the client becomes more and more emotionally detached from the process of his own recovery.

There are two people in the helping relationship, and the addict has lived his life with codependents. The addict's goal is to avoid taking responsibility for the addiction by involving someone else in "curing" him and then reacting against this control. The client is not responsible for setting limits in the relationship. We are. In not recognizing codependence, in not insisting that the client take responsibility for following through, we are enabling the client. Although it may not look like enabling because we are expressing an inordinate degree of anger toward the client, we are enablers nonetheless. If we are overly emotionally involved, then the client recognizes this and the old, familiar game plays on.

A more subtle form of professional codependence consists of our taking all the responsibility for treatment effectiveness and for taking treatment success and failure personally. Because our genuine role as helper does overlap with the "messiah," we need to be especially cautious about falling into the enabler trap. We do oppose and try to change the client's alcohol and drug use, and because of that we must also place responsibility on the patient for her recovery and whatever slips and relapses she has. There are actually many types of players within the "messiah" role. The common factor is that they all set out to change behavior, and then they inadvertently prevent the very change in behavior they seek by not allowing the client to feel the negative consequences of her behavior.

New counselors often fall into the trap of "helping the client out" with all sorts of things from cigarettes to large sums of money. The counselors look like they are being taken advantage of (and they are), but they defend themselves as just "being nice," "being there for him," and so on. The counselor takes the client places, buys her things, spends her free time with the client. Usually, this does not pay off because the client must take responsibility for her recovery. The client must work at it, and this is not easy. She must experience the losses caused by her drug use. If we keep picking the client up, how is she going to learn to pick herself up? How can the client build self-esteem and self-confidence if she is dependent on someone else for her recovery?

If we pay attention to the balance of the relationship, then we can detect the messiah in ourselves. Where possible, the client needs to do things for himself. He needs to make the phone calls, search for a job, and get himself to a meeting when he needs a meeting. Are we doing things for the client that he could do for himself to "make it easier" for him? The written treatment plan is extremely helpful in keeping the balance. The client must follow through with the goals and objectives on a weekly basis. Helping the client means not letting him off the hook when he fails to follow through.

Another sign that the counselor is playing the messiah role is his accepting the client's verbal abuse. Why would it be helpful to the client to allow him to swear or yell at the counselor? This may be typical for an angry teenager, but the goal is growth not regression. If you tolerate verbal abuse from your client because your client "needs" you, you may have learned from your parents that the only thing you are good for is to be a dumping ground for other people's anger. The client must learn how to take responsibility for his feelings and the handling of his feelings.

Just because we are not playing a "nice guy" role does not mean we are not codependent. We can play the "bad guy," the punisher, and still qualify for the role. One type or variant of codependence is the persecutor, according to Cermak (1986). The persecutor is the opposite of the martyr. Persecutors have a lot of rage, and they manipulate others with anger and guilt. A persecutor-type of counselor may attempt to control the client through anger and guilt. Why would a counselor yell at a patient? The counselor is codependent. If we are yelling at our patient, we need Al-Anon. We are trying to control the disease and the behavior of another, and we are angry at the client because we are unable to do that. The battle has nothing to do with the client, who happens to be sitting in the middle between us and our unresolved conflict. The client is a bystander in his own recovery.

The counselor's internal cues provide important clues that her co-dependence is active. Pay attention to your feelings. Does a particular patient bring up guilt feelings in you? Does this patient get you to do things for her that you do not do for other patients? Do you tell this patient things you do not tell others? Does a particular patient call you often with a crisis situation? Do you wish that this patient would not show up for an appointment? Do what we call "needy" patients always seem to be invading your space, making it more difficult than ever to maintain the proper boundaries and roles? What type of patient pushes your buttons? Do you work better with men than with women? With younger patients than with older ones? Be aware of your prejudices (ethnic, religious, gender, sexual preference) for they limit the quality of care that you can give a client.

Your feelings about your patients tell you a lot about yourself and about your patients. If you are "taking the patient home with you" emotionally, ask yourself what it is about this patient that causes that to happen. You probably need to increase the structure or limit your interactions with this client. Cut down on the client's phone calls as a goal of reducing the client's dependency on you. Limit your answers about personal information to ensure that the client is using the session to focus on himself and not on you. If you are "taking your patient home with you" physically, you need to seek counsel.

A final red flag indicating active codependence is taking over the management of the client's life medically, psychologically, and legally. This occurs with medical professionals. For example, a nurse may take the total care of the addicted individual into her own hands and act against the advice of the physician in charge because she "knows what is best" for the patient. The nurse may decide the patient has too much pain medication and holds back on that medication in order to "help" the addict not get hooked on the drug. She is attempting to control the patient's addiction and is inadvertently punishing the addict at the same time.

Professional codependence is, in fact, so common among health care providers that there is a book written for this group entitled *I'm Dying to Take Care of You* (Snow and Willard, 1990). The title conveys the problem: health care providers often put the needs of patients before their own to the detriment of everyone.

Some codependent medical professionals are of the persecutor type. Such physicians and nurses may respond less quickly to the "drunk" who needs help than to the person next to him. They are punishing the active alcoholic. The type of enabler (messiah, persecutor) does not appear to be determined by whether the professional helper is suffering from the disease of addiction himself. Helping professionals who are active alcoholics and those who are "recovered" are just as likely to be punishers as are helpers who do not have an addiction. Apparently persecutors have not dealt with their own rage and shame about the disease, and they take it out on the alcoholic who is "out of control." The disease they rage against may be their own or it may be that of a loved one (parent, spouse). The bedridden patient is an easy target for these unresolved feelings about the disease of addiction.

One physician in a treatment center for addictions refused to give a woman patient a hot water bottle because the physician said he would be "enabling" her. Physicians can be "co-conspirators," to use Cermak's term, in handing out all the medication a patient wants regardless of whether it is needed. Or, alternatively, the physician can be the persecutor in not prescribing needed medication because he has a "gut feeling" the patient is an addict. We need to recognize the difference between compassion and enabling. We need not to use the "enabling" concept as an excuse for punishing people we perceive as bad.

Some helpers in the addictions field either tell lies for their patients (to licensing boards, lawyers, family members, or police) or recommend that their patients lie. How much responsibility are we willing to take? How much control over the lives of our patients do we want to handle? Heed the A.A. slogans: Let it go, turn it over, we are not that powerful, we are not the patient's higher power. Every time we deceive someone on behalf of our patient, we are doing our client a disservice. We are telling our patient that it is okay to be dishonest, we are not showing faith in a higher power, we are taking moral responsibility for our patient. We are liable for the outcome. This is also true with simple advice. After the patient learns how to not use the addictive substance, no one can tell him what is best for him. Only the patient knows what is best for him, and he has to discover that for himself, with our guidance.

Advantages and Disadvantages
of Being a Recovering Counselor

Although I am not a recovering counselor myself, from my experience I can see several advantages to treating a disease from which one is recovering. Primarily, the clients feel so bad about themselves when they first enter treatment that they are more willing to talk openly with someone who is "like them" or "has been there." Some of my students who are in recovery say that if, when they first entered treatment, their counselor was not in recovery, they would not have talked to him. The counselor can serve as a role model for the recovering client; he gives the client hope by virtue of the fact that he is sober. The recovering counselor can come up with more practical solutions for day-to-day sober living than the nonrecovering counselor. The nonrecovering counselor has to learn this information through her counseling experience and peer supervision.

There are also disadvantages to being a recovering counselor. As an A.A. member or sponsor, you help the recovering person by sharing your own story and the person in turn identifies with your story. A different process occurs in counseling, where you typically go quickly beyond this sharing and identification format to focus on the client and his thoughts and feelings independent of yours. It is, however, very difficult for some counselors to switch roles or approaches, at least initially. They tend to focus too much on themselves rather than helping to develop the client's self, relying more heavily on the process of identification than on the process of empathy.

There is an important difference between empathy and identification. As Benjamin (1974), writes of this difference: "The empathic interviewer...tries to see the world through the [interviewee's] eyes as if that world were his own world.... Being there, he may be able to understand the interviewee; but it is only when he returns to himself, to his own life space, that he is able to help." In the process of identification, the client wishes to be just like the counselor. The counselor is asking the client to put himself in the counselor's shoes, to see things through the counselor's sober eyes. As Benjamin describes the client's view in this process, "I wish to erase myself and to substitute the self of the other." The loss of boundaries between the interviewee and the interviewer is called identification rather than empathy. Loss of boundaries increases the client's dependence on the counselor and decreases the client's sense of self-efficacy, his reliance on his own strengths and abilities.

The counselor's dependence on "her own story" in helping the patient get well has several effects. Personal information shared by the counselor may be used by the client to avoid taking responsibility for himself. He may use the information as a reason to invalidate the counselor by reasoning, "She's as sick as I am. Why should I listen to her?" The client may spend the session taking the focus off himself and focusing on the counselor's issues. The client may become intrusive with the information he has and continue to follow up on it in future sessions. He may require more and more of the counselor's time and attention in order to continue a "special" relationship. He may begin attending the counselor's meetings.

If you feel your privacy is being invaded or you feel shame or guilt about the counseling relationship, then chances are the boundaries are slipping away and you need to set them up again. You need to express verbally your observation of what you feel is happening in the relationship and then you need to set up new ground rules in which the responsibility and focus are on the client and not on yourself. Generally, as the counselors' experience and confidence in their counseling abilities increases, sharing of personal information by the counselor decreases and, consequently, boundary problems occur less often.

Education and self-analysis of our feelings and thoughts about clients help prevent counselor impairment. Additionally, we need skilled supervision. Peer support groups are also very helpful in allowing us to express our feelings about our clients and our relationships with them. Keeping the focus on the client and maintaining structure in time (weekly sessions) and place (treatment setting) help to keep proper boundaries in this powerful nonmutual relationship.

= S I X =

TWELVE STEP PRINCIPLES AND COGNITIVE THERAPY

Twelve Step Programs and Rational Recovery

For over seventeen years, I have treated addictions by a combination of Twelve Step programs (Alcoholics Anonymous, Al-Anon, Narcotics Anonymous, and so on) and rational-emotive therapy. So I was surprised to hear recently that Rational Recovery (which has its roots in rational-emotive therapy) is being perceived not only as an alternative to A.A. but as critical of A.A. This feedback comes from my students who attended Rational Recovery (R.R.) groups in the Boston area. The students reported that much of the time was spent "A.A. bashing" with angry expressions regarding the spiritual component of A.A. In response, A.A. members are spending time and energy bashing Rational Recovery, albeit outside of A.A. meetings.

There is a basic difference between A.A. and R.R. A.A. uses a spiritual component; R.R. does not. A.A. is based on the Twelve Steps, reprinted in appendix A (p. 167). "Rational Recovery is an alternative to A.A. that doesn't have anything to do with any kind of higher power or spiritual aspects of recovery. It uses RET in its self-help groups" (Albert Ellis, letter to the author, May 1991). As previously noted, rational-emotive therapy was begun by Ellis back in the 1950s. Over the years, Ellis came up with techniques for treating addictions. In the 1970s he came out with a tape entitled *"I'd Quit but..." Dealing with Addictions,* and in 1988 he coauthored a very good counseling guide for treating addictions with rational-emotive techniques. Although Ellis has always made it clear that he is an atheist, only when the R.R.

movement became more vocal did the God-factor become a point of conflict.

In comparing these two self-help group formats from an outsider's perspective, I believe there are "human factors" that need to be taken into account: (1) the difference between a philosophy in the abstract or ideal sense and the way that the philosophy is actually put into practice by human beings, and (2) the tendency to misinterpret or misrepresent the other group's philosophy. On the first issue, let me say that both R.R. and A.A. are practiced very differently from their stated purposes and principles. For instance, R.R. groups are reported to be disorganized and to spend a great deal of time putting down the A.A. program. A.A. members are no more likely to always live the Twelve Step principles than are churchgoers likely to always live Christian lives. What I find, generally, is that group members take what they need and leave the rest.

The second issue, and the more emotionally charged one, is the misinterpretation of program philosophy. Jack Trimpey (1990), director of Rational Recovery Systems, in my opinion, misinterprets the A.A. philosophy. He says that in coming to A.A. millions of alcoholics and other substance abusers learn that "they are wrong in what they think and believe, in the ways they act, and in how they perceive themselves. They learn to their chagrin that they are wrong about the very meaning of life, and about the contents of the universe itself." My first reaction to this criticism is to recognize it as precisely the same as that voiced over the years against the RET approach. RET and, thus, R.R. teach the person a new philosophy of life. In fact, I know of no other system of therapy that more aggressively attacks and changes people's faulty belief systems. The goal of changing the belief systems is to change the person's feelings and behaviors. If anything, A.A. would seem to be less aggressive in its attempts to change the individual. The individual in A.A. listens and chooses a pathway. In RET and R.R., people are directed toward changing beliefs, feelings, and behavior. Trimpey fails to see the similarities between R.R. and A.A. philosophies.

The difference between A.A. and R.R. is the spiritual component. Trimpey (1990) writes about A.A.'s message to addicts: "For example, a substance abuser who decides, 'I want to beat this thing; I really think I can do it,' is urged to think instead, 'I can't do it myself. I am powerless over my addiction.'" A.A. does not say that the person is powerless over his addiction; A.A. says the person is powerless over alcohol. When the person is actively drinking alcohol, he loses control over the substance and over his life. Admitting his powerlessness over alcohol is the first step in his taking responsibility for his behavior. I do not think any aspect of recovery is more crucial to recovery than the person recognizing that he or she has lost control over alcohol.

Contrary to Trimpey's statements, R.R. is certainly advocating that the person has lost control over alcohol by virtue of the fact that the person is taught how not to drink. If the person really can gain control over alcohol, then why doesn't R.R. teach drinking in moderation? Now that would be evidence of control over addiction! Moreover, we need to be careful about selectively quoting members, many of whom have their own hidden agendas or simply do not understand the principles of the program. Anyone who has taught a class or counseled people knows that people "hear" things that are never said. There is a saying in A.A. that speaks to this phenomenon: "You hear what you want to hear." I have clients who say that A.A. members force their religion on them. This may be true, but it is certainly not the way A.A. was meant to be and it is certainly not the way most members or most meetings operate. If I believed that all R.R. groups were run the way my students described them (from their perspective as A.A. members), I would never refer a client to them. It is always wise in the field of recovery to consider the source, but not to dismiss it, when weighing the information.

Let me make one final comment on this issue of self-reliance versus reliance on others. Trimpey (1990) states:

> There is no sponsor or buddy system in RR because these arrangements support the belief that one is personally powerless and must depend on something other than or greater than oneself in order to refuse alcohol or drugs. Instead of calling a sponsor in a time of temptation, members simply write.... At the next meeting, the tempted one will have an opportunity to get group feedback.

In response to this statement, I feel compelled to ask: What is the difference between choosing to call a sponsor for help and bringing one's problem back to the group for help? True, the member has delayed asking for help, but he is still dependent on the group. "Self-help group" is really a contradiction in terms. If it were self-help, then you would not have a group. If a sponsor is a form of dependency, then so too are self-help groups as are group therapists, individual counselors, mentors, and the like.

Is it really so important that we perceive ourselves as not wanting or needing help from others? A.A. does not teach its members to be dependent any more than RET teaches people not to feel. Some people will use the philosophies in these ways, but that is not the intent. A.A. did not make such people dependent, and RET did not make them nonemotional; these people have found a way to fit a system into their preexisting perceptions of reality in order not to change. A.A. can help people get sober; it does not necessarily make people less dependent. For some, A.A. is the only "family" or social system they have. I do not think that a dependent person would be made less dependent through a short-term R.R. group.

Let us now turn to the real point of conflict between these two programs: the spiritual aspect. Treatment options are needed for the millions of active alcoholics; however, it is not clear whether there are active alcoholics who do not use A.A. *because of* the spiritual component and whether offering a nonspiritual option would increase the number of recovered addicts. In 1978, Maultsby stated that "alcoholics prefer self-help treatment methods to those of traditional health professionals, *but* less than 20 percent of America's 20+ million alcoholics accept A.A.'s self-help treatment." In my opinion, the fact that 80 percent of America's alcoholics reject all forms of treatment says more about the qualities of the disease (e.g., denial) than the qualities of treatment options. The active alcoholic does not believe alcohol is a problem, so why should she seek help for a problem that does not exist? If someone offered a treatment approach that allowed alcoholics to continue drinking alcohol, I have the feeling that the percentage of alcoholics in treatment would dramatically increase.

When it comes to the issue of self-control, we continue to get bogged down in semantics. Trimpey (1990) writes about R.R., "Members are helped to recognize that they certainly do have control over their actions and, in fact, have been in control of their substance abuse all along — in control, but making consistently bad decisions." This statement denies the power of unconscious processes and the power of physical addiction. The active alcoholic does not even know he is making a decision. He simply does not have a problem with booze. Does Trimpey really believe that a fifteen-year-old heroin addict in the projects is making a decision to shoot heroin into her veins? Did Kitty Dukakis, wife of the governor of Massachusetts, make a decision to drink rubbing alcohol? If she were just choosing to drink alcohol, she would have grabbed a bottle off the top shelf. Does the drunk on the street decide to take a swig of whiskey to reduce tremors? How can you make a bad choice when you do not yet know you have a choice?

We do not have to crush one self-help program to justify the need for a second one. There are plenty of active addicts to go around. The more alternative forms of treatment available, the more likely we are to increase the percentage of recovering addicts. Ellis reports that there are now over 150 Rational Recovery self-help groups in the country. This fact supports the idea that an alternative self-help format is needed, although we might note that 150 self-help groups or, approximately fifteen hundred members, represents a relatively small fraction of the 20 million alcoholics.

The success of R.R. groups in attracting addicts does not prove one way or another that the spiritual component of recovery is nonessential. Alcoholics may be attracted to R.R. groups for other reasons. For instance, unlike A.A., R.R. groups are time-limited and thus the recovering alcoholic does not need to address emotionally the fact that he is suffering from a disease that he will need to attend to for the rest of his life.

R.R.'s success in attracting members does not speak to the issue of a spirituality in recovery. However, logically, we know that not everyone needs to believe in a God in order to live a healthy, satisfying life, and not every recovering addict needs to believe in a higher power in order to have a quality recovery. As living proof of this logic are those happily recovered individuals who do not believe in a higher power.

From my experience, the most effective treatment is one that uses philosophies of both RET and the Twelve Step principles through individual and group processes. Spirituality is a dimension of our being, and recognizing that dimension furthers our experience of life. Obviously, those who do not believe in a spiritual aspect of self are not going to focus on the development of that aspect. Aside from the spiritual aspect, both Twelve Step programs and RET are aimed at making philosophical changes in the individual. Twelve Step programs do this through a self-help format, and RET does this typically through individual and group counseling methods. Twelve Step programs focus on developing one's relationship with another, a higher power, and a group of recovering individuals. Rational-emotive therapy focuses on one's beliefs about alcohol and drugs, about self, and about others. Twelve Step programs and cognitive behavioral therapy both have an essential behavioral component. In A.A., you hear about someone "talking but not walking the program" and "needing to do the legwork." Both approaches require some behavioral changes as proof of philosophical change.

Rational-emotive therapy urges us to accept our nonperfection as a reality; so do the Twelve Step programs. You can accept that you are not perfect without asking God to remove your imperfections. Accepting our limitations and then turning over our will are two different but complementary processes. My experience as an addictions therapist leads me to conclude that believing in a higher power further advances the client's recovery. If people turn their will over to God, does that mean that they give up responsibility for their lives? Of course not. It simply means they recognize that they will not always get what they want and that there is a greater plan of which they are a part. It means they do not always have to be in the driver's seat. On the other hand, from a nonspiritual perspective, people can learn to give up control over that which they recognize rationally they cannot control without believing there is a power greater than themselves in control of that element. For instance, you can stop blaming yourself for the death of your child without believing that "God has a plan and everything happens for a reason."

There are also some pros and cons to these approaches that have to do with what we know to be true of the disease of addiction and its treatment. When we put ourselves in the powerful position of deciding which approach would benefit which client, we run the risk of limiting the client's growth. For instance, some very intellectual and educated types are going to tell their counselors that they will not go to A.A., not because they do not believe in God but because "I do not want to sit in a room full of drunks and listen to their drunkalogues all night." On the other hand, insisting to an alcoholic that she must attend A.A. or she will never get sober when she has already stated that she will never go to A.A. is just as defeating of recovery.

Limiting self-help attendance to those groups that we personally believe in may short-circuit the recovery process. It may be that addiction is a disease in which we do not know necessarily what the client is going to respond to on a less than conscious level. We enter the same arena of risk here that we enter when we send physicians to Physicians Only groups or nurses to Nurses Only groups. These special groups for professionals may not cut through the denial that is evident in beliefs such as: "I am better than them. I have a different disease than they have. I am not that bad. I am not an addict. I can learn to drink socially." These faulty beliefs are not going to be changed solely through intellectualization. They are going to be changed experientially: going to the meetings, sitting with "the drunks," and beginning to feel that you do share their disease. On the other hand, there are benefits to these special groups. The members can talk about how to deal with what are "occupational hazards" for the addict returning to the workplace, for instance, how to limit access to medication or how it feels to have such huge quantities of drugs available to them. I recommend to the recovering medical professionals with whom I work that they try both types of meetings.

A second danger of restricting treatment to a rational approach with a group of alcoholics and drug abusers is that, as anyone who works with addicts knows, there is a fine line between rationalization as a defense and rational thought as a treatment method. Addicted individuals are, by their nature, some of the world's greatest rationalizers, a.k.a. con artists. They have more reasons for drinking, for not quitting, for why drinking was not their fault, why it was not that bad, ad infinitum, than counselors can imagine. Getting them to *stop* being "in their heads," i.e., rationalizing, and to start feeling is the challenge.

Another potential danger inherent in using only R.R. is that the group ends after a limited period of time. People recover at different rates; for many it is a lifelong process. Will some alcoholics feel they have failed if they do not gain sobriety by the end of the group meetings? Moreover, there is something positive and generational about the fact that A.A. has been around for sixty years and continues to grow and will always be there if you need it. People form lifelong friendships in A.A., and they go on to help others get sober as part of their recovery. We must always remember, however, that "what works works." A.A. is not for everyone, nor is Rational Recovery. We need to try out different approaches to see what works best for the individual client.

Alcoholics Anonymous also has its drawbacks when it is utilized as the sole approach to recovery. In particular, some of the A.A. slogans begin to be misused by some within the fellowship. The belief "Let go, let God" can become an excuse to not move forward and work to achieve what one wants and needs in life. The belief that "this is a selfish program" is sometimes used in later recovery as an excuse for not developing mutual relationships. There is also a belief that "civilians" (nonaddicts) do not understand "us" and therefore members limit their socialization only to those in A.A. and develop a sense of mistrust for "outsiders." There is also a tendency for the program to become "my life" rather than "a part of my life." A.A. becomes a place to hide out from life. Such rigid and self-limiting beliefs make for a very narrow experience of humankind.

The usefulness of self-help groups has to do with the qualities of the recovering person. Some "high-bottom addicts" — those who have not had a lot of losses, who are probably younger and better educated, and who have a briefer addiction history — may be able to use R.R. just as effectively as A.A. On the other hand, I find it difficult to believe that some of the low-bottom addicts, especially those with cognitive damage, will be able to get sober and maintain their sobriety using a cognitively based, didactic, short-term group. In my private practice, I have found that the older, late-stage alcoholic is less able to use RET than is the younger, early-stage alcoholic. R.R. may be more helpful with types of nonchemical addiction in which the goal is moderate use (e.g., food, sex) than with addictions requiring abstinence (e.g., chemicals or gambling).

A.A. has organized itself over the course of nearly seventy years; R.R. self-help groups are only in their beginning phase of development. As they develop, the boundaries of the group will become clearer.

With such boundaries, the disturbances, such as disgruntled ex-A.A. members expressing their anger at A.A., will lessen. Rational Recovery groups will not be perceived as a forum for A.A.-bashers and thus will not attract them. In time, the antagonism between the two self-help groups will lessen just as it has between A.A. and Al-Anon. Rational Recovery appears to be a viable option for those individuals who wish to get sober but, for whatever reason, do not seem to get anything out of the A.A. self-help group.

Integration

Since both A.A. and cognitive therapy are optimal for different aspects of the self, the real question is how to integrate the two approaches. The recovering person ideally is always working on three aspects of self: cognitive, spiritual, and emotional/relational. The focus shifts from one aspect to another, depending on where the person is in recovery.

The client works on challenging an irrational belief system primarily by learning cognitive techniques in counseling, but he also learns to develop rational self-help statements in Twelve Step programs. The client works on his spiritual self primarily in A.A., but also shares this with his counselor at times. The emotional aspect has to do with feelings about self and others. I refer to this as the relational aspect because it is dealt with primarily in the client's relationship with his counselor.

The point of intersection of these two approaches can be seen in A.A. slogans such as "One day at a time" and "Keep it simple." Both cognitive behavioral therapy, in particular RET, and Twelve Step programs stress philosophical changes, supported by various self-instructional slogans.

This points up the important connection between changing patterns of automatic thoughts and more general beliefs and successful recovery from addiction. "What alcoholics and other addicts tell themselves about their problem, the feeling they experience in trying to deal with their problem, and, most importantly, what they tell themselves about themselves for having their problem are the key beliefs that RET aims at helping clients change" (Ellis et al., 1988). The same can be said for Twelve Step programs.

Cognitive behavioral techniques are very important in changing a person's irrational belief system. For instance, there are irrational beliefs that are specific to drinking and drugging, such as: "I must have a drink if I feel badly," "I cannot stand feeling angry!" "Drinking will make me feel better." Then there are some more general irrational beliefs we need to work on with the client later in recovery: beliefs and expectations that the client has of himself and others. For instance, the client's demanding that others love and care for him: "You are my mother and therefore *you must* love and accept me!" Cognitive behavioral techniques are very effective in changing such beliefs.

What, then, are Twelve Step programs for? The Twelve Steps are a philosophy of life, the whole of it. Cognitive behavioral techniques can help get rid of, or reduce, feelings of self-loathing, guilt, anger, and shame, but they really do not tell one how to work through the valid feelings of anger, sadness, and hurt. For instance, clients can come to accept that their mothers did not love them and not feel a burning rage about that, but they are still left with the very legitimate feelings of sadness and hurt. Clients learn how to deal with their feelings about selves and loved ones through a relationship with another: a higher power, and a counselor who provides a sense of safety and guidance.

Books on counseling the recovering person tell us about the techniques and tasks used in helping some get and stay sober, but they do not tell us a whole lot about the relational or relationship aspects. The client needs to recognize the strengths she has and develop those she does not have, strengths such as trust or faith in herself and others. Often we are not doing rehabilitation; we are doing habilitation. We are aiding in the development of a person, not simply stopping an addictive behavior.

Cognitive behavioral techniques are not complete in this sense because they speak primarily to the cognitive aspect of the person. If A.A. provides an introduction and forum for having a relationship with a higher power, then the counseling relationship provides a forum for having a relationship with self and others.

In both Twelve Step programs and the developmental cognitive behavioral approach I use, the recovering person focuses first on self in admitting powerlessness. He then focuses on self in relation to a higher power and then on self in relation to others. In terms of his belief system, the client first challenges his irrational beliefs specific to alcohol-

and drug-related behavior, then his beliefs in relation to himself, and finally his beliefs in relation to others. Practically all of these beliefs have to do with the issues of control and power.

The Twelve Step Tradition and Cognitive Counseling

The Twelve Steps are now used as a foundation in other self-help programs (Co-Dependents Anonymous, Overeaters Anonymous, Gamblers Anonymous, Sex and Love Addicts Anonymous, to name a few). The Steps, as used in A.A., are listed in appendix A (p. 167). The substance or behavior is simply changed to fit the type of self-help meeting. The first three steps are about admitting and accepting powerlessness. These steps are stated as follows:

> We admitted we were powerless over alcohol — that our lives had become unmanageable.

> Came to believe that a Power greater than ourselves could restore us to sanity.

> Made a decision to turn our will and our lives over to the care of God *as we understood Him.*

The next four steps are about admitting and accepting one's imperfection as a human being:

> Made a searching and fearless moral inventory of ourselves.

> Admitted to God, to ourselves, and to another human being the exact nature of our wrongs.

> Were entirely ready to have God remove all these defects of character.

> Humbly asked Him to remove our shortcomings.

Steps Eight through Ten talk about making mistakes in relation to others and making amends for that harm:

> Made a list of all persons we had harmed, and became willing to make amends to them all.

Made direct amends to such people wherever possible....

Continued to take personal inventory and when we were wrong promptly admitted it.

Steps Eleven and Twelve deal with furthering one's relationship with God and then carrying his message to others in the program.

Step One involves admitting powerlessness. In counseling, I ask the client to complete a Step One exercise. In this exercise, the client makes a list of those behaviors that demonstrate her loss of control over drinking or drugging. The client must then list ways in which her drinking hurt her relationship with significant others. There are both cognitive and relational aspects to this exercise. Admitting that she lost control over her compulsive behavior will help her break through the denial that allows her to believe that she can return to the moderate use of the addictive substance. When people relapse, it is usually through that insidious belief that "maybe I can have just one." Hopefully, the person has changed that irrational belief by continually convincing herself that she did lose control and when she did lose control, she lost. She lost herself, her friends, her family, her finances, and so on.

What is the relational aspect of this step? If the person is in counseling and not only attending A.A., then this step involves trusting one's counselor and having some faith that the counselor knows how to help. Asking for help is an important step because it acknowledges that the addicted individual does not have to do it alone, and it risks trusting another person to help and guide him in the right direction.

For a while, the relational aspect involves the counselor's doing some parenting type of work with her clients. We acknowledge their pain, and we respond with empathy. We offer the unconditional acceptance they lack, and we teach them self-acceptance. We respond positively as their sober days increase, and we encourage them to seek out a support system in A.A. with a sponsor and new sober friends. And, eventually, we let go.

What is the spiritual aspect of this step? Admitting on an emotional level that the addict has no control over a substance is a big step. Admitting that she is vulnerable and needs help is a necessary step to recovery. The person must believe and feel on a gut level that she is powerless against this drug or behavior. This is contrary to all that went before:

The "I don't need your help" attitude, the lack of vulnerability, the feeling of power, and the egocentricity. In my experience, very few clients refuse to *try* to ask a higher power for help, and the more they try to communicate with their higher power, the greater is their belief in a higher power.

Step Two involves coming "to believe that a Power greater than ourselves...." Recovering people tend to operate in extremes. This makes sense, for isn't an addiction a philosophy of "You can't just have one — be it a drink, a cookie, or a gambling bet"? Their belief in their own power is extreme as well, more extreme than for the nonrecovering person. People in Twelve Step programs grew up believing they were powerful, and this is as true for the nonaddicted adult child as it is for the chemically addicted person. They believe that they *should* have the power to change all manner of things. They believe that they *should* be great achievers. They believe that they are responsible for the pain and the happiness of others.

Within a cognitive framework, Step Two involves the client's acknowledging that she does not run the universe, she cannot control all manner of things, and she especially cannot control a behavior over which she has admittedly lost control — be it alcohol, drugs, gambling, food, or relationships. If the client gives up this illusion of control, which is making her "insane," she will, in fact, return to sanity.

The spiritual aspect adds to this understanding of the idea that there is something greater than oneself. There is someone or something out there who is going to lead the way, is going to help if the person gives up the illusion of power. The spiritual aspect involves having faith that someone knows better than they do what is good for them. This may not be a "someone"; it may be a belief in, say, universality. It is a belief that there is some positive master plan or organizing principle for the universe.

The relational aspect, again, involves trust, hope, and faith in the relationship between the client and the counselor. From that basis, the client is able to move forward and risk developing friendships in A.A. The client learns that she does not have to isolate, that there are people out there with whom she can have friendships. We can argue that only if the client comes to trust in someone or something (counselor, higher power) can she give up the need to be in control of the universe.

Step Three involves actually turning one's will over to a higher power. I find that many clients say they turn their will over, but then when things do not go their way, they quickly take it back, which means, of course, that they never really turned it over in the first place. Step Three is a long process. Most clients can turn over their will with regard to the use of chemicals, but in other areas, such as intimate relationships, they have difficulty in trusting their higher power.

The idea that "everything happens for a reason" is one the client hears in A.A., and it is also a cognitive self-statement. This self-statement is made to challenge the irrational belief that "I *must* get what I want when I want it!" Such childish demandingness leads to overwhelming irrational feelings of anger and hurt that, in turn, lead to a drink or a drug. The spiritual aspect of this slogan or cognitive self-statement is the implicit belief that everything happens for a reason *because* there is a power greater than us who knows what is best for us. Relationally, this step involves trust: trusting that the counselor will help and not hurt, will accept and not reject (even having heard all one's "terrible" secrets), and knowing that one is becoming *trustworthy* by staying sober.

The next four steps focus on the fact that people are not perfect. This is also an essential step in RET. Rational-emotive therapy teaches that we need to admit and accept that we are fallible human beings who are not perfect and who make mistakes. If we are not perfect, if we do make mistakes, that does not make us bad and worthless; it just makes us human. These four steps also involve going beyond challenging perfectionistic beliefs to admitting them to God and to another person, and then being open to having them taken away by God.

Steps Eight and Nine expand the person's recovery by involving other human beings in the process. In these steps, the recovering person admits to those he has hurt that he is aware that he has hurt them and has feelings about that. This is called making amends.

The client is always working on the cognitive, the spiritual, and the emotional/relational aspects of self. After the first year, concerns shift from not drinking today to getting along with others in mutually satisfying relationships. The client is learning in A.A. the limits of her power, she is learning to have faith in a God, and she is learning to develop sober friendships and to utilize a mentor. In her counseling relationship the client is learning to risk trusting self and others through sharing feelings and secrets.

The client in the second year of recovery is also learning to accept the limitations of others. As the client turns toward relationships, the real struggle with feelings about self and trust in others begins. For those who have given up the control of chemicals must now recognize that they cannot control the behavior of others. They cannot make others love them. They cannot get their children or parents sober. They cannot make their spouses happy. In accepting these limitations of loved ones, they are painfully accepting their own limitations. No matter how perfect they are or, alternatively, how dysfunctional they are, they cannot control others' feelings and behaviors.

Clients who cannot (will not) let go of their perceived control over a loved one probably need to go back and work Step Three. At this point of frustration with love relationships, we often see relapse or a return to other obsessive-compulsive behaviors: food, sex, smoking. The person does not feel safe (trust) enough to give up control. These behaviors are clear signs that clients need more work on their spiritual and relational selves.

In summary, in this chapter I have shown the strengths and weaknesses of the cognitive behavioral and Twelve Step program approaches to addictions. I have also suggested how the two systems overlap and complement each other and how they can be integrated to create the most effective treatment approach.

WHAT'S NEW IN TREATMENT?

*A Cognitive-Behavioral-Twelve Step Approach
to Alcohol and Other Drugs*

A significant development in the field of addiction over the past decade has been the growth of addiction-specific approaches, or, more accurately, the application of broad treatment models or approaches to addictions and, even more specifically, to a certain drug such as heroin or cocaine. My goal is to present counseling techniques in a way that is interesting and useable and does not overwhelm the student. I hope to achieve this goal by reducing the technical jargon as much as possible and distilling these many approaches into a single approach containing the most effective ingredients.

What is common to all the accepted addictions approaches is that they are cognitive (identifying and challenging faulty beliefs that maintain the addiction), behavioral (we expect to see concrete changes), and they recognize the importance of the client-counselor or therapeutic relationship. Before launching into this comparison of current approaches, let me set the stage by presenting a few facts. The first set of facts presents the latest outcome of research on addictions treatment, and the news is positive. The second set of facts look at the current trends in use, and they are less than positive. But taken together, these facts provide the most current picture we have on substance dependence and treatment.

In 1997 the results were reported of a nationwide study that examined the effectiveness of four common types of drug abuse treatment, with all four types showing significant reductions in drug use. This research followed more than ten thousand patients in nearly a hundred programs in eleven cities. Drug use dropped significantly during the period beginning twelve months before treatment began and ending twelve months after treatment began. This was true for all four types of treatment studied:

- Outpatient methadone programs administer methadone to reduce cravings for heroin and block its effects. Counseling, vocational skills development, and case management help patients access support services. Some patients stay on methadone, while others become methadone abstinent.

- Long-term residential programs offer around-the-clock, drug-free treatment in a residential community of counselors and fellow recovering addicts. Patients generally stay in these programs several months or up to a year or more. Some of these programs are referred to as therapeutic communities (TCs).

- Outpatient drug-free programs use a wide range of approaches including problem-solving groups, specialized therapies, and Twelve Step programs. Patients may stay in these programs for months or longer.

- Short-term inpatient programs keep patients up to thirty days. Most of these programs focus on medical stabilization, abstinence, and lifestyle changes. Staff members are primarily medical professionals and trained counselors. Once primarily for alcohol abuse treatment, these programs expanded into drug abuse treatment in the 1980s.

This research is especially interesting because it follows up on two earlier studies, and therefore we can look for trends in treatment over the past thirty years. The first study, called the Drug Abuse Reporting Program (DARP), included admissions to treatment from 1969 to 1973. The second study, called the Treatment Outcomes Prospective Study (TOPS), covered admissions from 1979 to 1981. The current study covers admissions between 1991 and 1993. Here are a few of the highlights:

- Except in outpatient methadone programs, cocaine was the primary drug of abuse, with alcohol running a close second. Cocaine abuse was common even in outpatient methadone treatment programs for heroin addicts.

- There was a reduction after treatment in illegal acts, an increase in employment, and a decrease in suicidal thoughts and suicide attempts.

- Patients reported that it took them about seven years after they first used their primary drug to enter treatment.

- Even short-term inpatient treatment programs (no more than thirty days) yielded significant declines in drug use.

- The prevalence of co-occurring psychological disorders was high, especially for antisocial personality disorder (APD) — a pattern of disregard for the rights of others, irresponsibility, and lack of remorse — and major depression.

- Predictors of treatment completion included high motivation; legal pressure to stay in treatment; no prior trouble with the law; getting psychological counseling while in treatment; and a lack of other psychological problems, especially antisocial personality disorder.

In 1995, there were nearly 1.9 million admissions to publicly funded substance abuse treatments, according to data collected by the National Institute of Drug Abuse (NIDA).

- About 54 percent were alcohol treatment admissions; nearly 46 percent were for illicit drug abuse treatment.

- The largest number of illicit drug treatment admissions were for cocaine (38.3 percent), followed by heroin (25.5 percent), and marijuana (19.1 percent).

- Men made up about 70 percent of individuals in treatment; women 30 percent.

- Fifty-six percent were white, followed in number by African Americans (26 percent), Hispanics (7.7 percent), Native Americans (2.2), and Asians and Pacific Islanders (0.6 percent).

The most significant change since the writing of the first edition of this book is the increase in illicit drug use, and in response to this shift, I have expanded on the treatment of drugs other than alcohol. In an effort to offer to my students the most current and effective addictions counseling approach, I reviewed the approaches deemed most effective by NIDA based on research outcomes. The current manuals presented by NIDA are for cocaine abuse and dependence. NIDA chose to sponsor studies for different cocaine treatment approaches because of the increasing and significant health and social problems caused by cocaine abuse and addiction. The approaches obviously are applicable to other drugs as well.

At the outset the number of new strategies appeared overwhelming; however, when I compared the content of these approaches I saw that they are very similar and utilize most of the same components. The core of these approaches is cognitive, behavioral, and motivational techniques. The approaches are adapted to target a single drug (e.g., cocaine) or approach (e.g., group or individual). They are sometimes labeled as "manuals" and the user is encouraged to follow the manual.

The positive thing about a manual, which is like a cookbook, is that everyone adds the same amounts of the same ingredients, and therefore we can compare approaches and get an idea of which is the most effective. The negative side of this strategy is that it is not realistic. Most counselors, those who are not being studied, will vary the recipe, giving it their own personal flavor and thus rendering the research outcomes not applicable. I think the good news is this: the ingredients are simple, few, and effective even when taken out of the manual. If you use these tried and true techniques (establishing rapport, cognitive-behavioral-motivational techniques, Twelve Steps), whether in an individual or a group setting, you will be an effective counselor.

Let us first examine how the current "cognitive behavioral coping skills treatment" approach compares with the cognitive and Twelve Step approach presented in the last chapter. One "new approach" is that of Carroll (1998), who uses a short-term, focused approach to help cocaine-dependent individuals abstain from cocaine and other substances (Carroll, 1998; her NIDA manual is available online at www.nida.nih.gov/TXManuals/CBT1.html). CBT in this case is an acronym for "cognitive behavioral coping skills treatment," not the cognitive behavioral therapy with which we are familiar.

In this CBT approach, the term "cocaine abuser" or "cocaine-dependent person" is used to refer to persons who meet DSM-IV criteria for cocaine abuse or dependence. The author writes, "Very simply put, CBT attempts to help patients recognize, avoid, and cope." While the author attempts to differentiate this approach from others, and there may be some surface differences, it is essentially the cognitive behavioral approach as described by Aaron Beck or Albert Ellis. Active ingredients include functional analysis and skills training.

Functional analysis is simply helping the patient identify thoughts, feelings, and circumstances before and after cocaine use. Or, as Ellis, says, "A functional analysis involves helping clients see that their negative emotions are not serving their best long-term interests" (Ellis et al., 1988). Functional analysis helps the person identify high-risk situations or triggers. Skills training focuses first on abstaining (identifying high-risk situations, coping with thoughts about cocaine) and then broadens to include areas such as social isolation and unemployment. Coping is intrapersonal (e.g., coping with craving) and interpersonal (e.g., refusing offers of cocaine).

In addition, Carroll's CBT includes a motivational component. The person does a "decisional analysis," which is simply looking at the pros and cons of using a substance. The technique of decisional analysis is variously labeled in the addictions literature as cognitive or as motivational. It is both.

More illustrative is the description of what Carroll's CBT recipe is not. Approaches not part of CBT are listed as confrontation style, encouraging or even requiring attendance at self-help meetings, use of the disease model, and rational-emotive therapy. I would have to argue again that the active ingredients (the ones that make the recipe work) are cognitive behavioral, and rational-emotive therapy *is* cognitive behavioral. In fact, you can find the cognitive strategies listed in Carroll's manual in either Beck or Ellis.

The author goes on to state that her approach is most similar to other cognitive and behavioral therapies. These include Beck's cognitive therapy (Beck et al., 1991), the community reinforcement approach (CRA) (Azrin, 1976; Meyers and Smith, 1995), and Marlatt's relapse

prevention (Marlatt and Gordon, 1985). The community reinforcement approach "is a broad-spectrum behavioral treatment approach
for substance abuse problems ... that utilizes social, recreational, famil-
ial, and vocational reinforcers to aid clients in the recovery process"
(Meyers and Smith, 1995). Given that the main ingredients in her recipe
are found in the cookbooks of both Beck and Ellis, it is hard to understand how her approach differs from Ellis but not from Beck. The
difference between Ellis and Beck, I would suggest, is that Ellis adds
more seasoning to his recipe, and if you have ever seen him in action
you would know this to be true.

Carroll also states that a confrontational style, self-help meeting attendance, and use of the disease model are not part of her approach. She
attempts to make the argument that her CBT is not compatible with
Twelve Step principles, which includes the disease concept. She states,
"The disease-model approaches are grounded in a concept of addiction
as a disease that can be controlled but never cured. In CBT, substance
abuse is a learned behavior that can be modified." Is she suggesting that
a person who is substance dependent can, with treatment, become a
"social user" of a substance?

These two beliefs are not incompatible: one can believe that substance abuse behavior is both learned and a disease. In fact, nearly all
authors of the most current approaches — even the scientists at NIDA —
believe that addiction is a disease. Believers in the Twelve Step principles
certainly believe that substance abuse behavior can be modified. And
I don't see any clinical researchers arguing for controlled or moderate
drinking; the consensus is that you can modify your behavior but that
will not allow you to return to drinking because there is no cure for this
disease. Further she argues that the focus of the disease model approach
is on patients' loss of control over substance abuse and other aspects
of their lives; the emphasis in CBT is on self-control strategies. In fact,
in the DSM-IV the core criterion of alcohol or drug dependence is loss
of control over the substance. This is the accepted behavioral definition of alcohol or drug dependence: continued use despite losses, use of
more of a substance than intended, and so forth. Why would we need to
teach people control strategies if they had not lost control? Both CBT
and TSF (Twelve Step Facilitation) teach control strategies.

She states that "the major change agent in disease-model approaches is involvement with the fellowship of AA/CA and working the twelve steps, that is, the way to cope with nearly all drug-related problems is by going to a meeting.... In CBT, coping strategies are much more individualized and based on specific types of problems encountered by patients and their usual coping style." This statement highlights the main problem with so many different manuals and approaches labeled idiosyncratically by the authors: it confuses and overwhelms the student. What underlies all these individualized coping strategies is very simple: cognitive theory. These manuals are technical, sometimes at the cost of depth of understanding. If you teach a client or counselor the theory and method (e.g., cognitive theory and ABCDs), you do not have to be at his side telling him how he is to respond to each and every faulty belief, unmanageable feeling, or high-risk situation. If we are to spend large sums of money on clinical research, the goal should be to produce something that is actually put into practice by treatment providers so that it may benefit the patients.

The beauty of Twelve Step principles is an understanding of this fact. The Twelve Step approach is not technical; it has depth. As the authors of the manual on individual drug counseling write, "Twelve-step ideology offers patients seeking recovery a new modus vivendi, or way of living, that will support them in breaking the cycle of addiction and maintaining abstinence.... The strengths and usefulness of the 12-step approach seem to have several sources.... Procedurally virtually any presenting situation can be dealt with effectively by applying the appropriate lesson or lessons" (Mercer and Woody, 1999; the manual is available online at www.nida.nih.gov/TXManuals/IDCA/IDCA1.html).

Perhaps progress is shown in Dr. Carroll's concluding remark that "CBT therapists take a neutral stance to attending AA," and A.A. is listed as a compatible adjunctive treatment. Given that when the adjunct of A.A. is added (and participation encouraged) the effectiveness of the treatment is increased, clinicians should seriously consider understanding Twelve Step principles, explaining them to their clients, and encouraging participation.

Another essential component of addictions counseling can be elaborated on through analysis of Carroll's CBT approach: confrontation. She states that hers is not a "confrontational style." In fact, it is not at all clear what she means by "confrontational style," and she is not alone in this. The term "confrontation" has negative connotations, but most, if not all, addictions counselors would agree that confrontation is essential for change. Carroll does not see her approach as confrontational, although she does use confrontation. She writes, "Confronting patients about discrepancies in self versus laboratory reports of substance use is very important; done well, this can advance the therapeutic relationship and the process of treatment significantly. However, pointing out these discrepancies should not be done in a confrontational style. Rather, therapists might point out discrepancies between the patients' stated treatment goals and the urine results (You've said things are all going great, but the urine results make me wonder if it's as easy as you say. What do you make of this?)." This confrontation style or method is commonly used: presenting the client with a contradiction or discrepancy between what he says (or does) now and has said or done (at another point in time).

The theory most associated with this type of confrontation today is motivational interviewing (Miller and Rollnick, 2002), presented in the next chapter. However, it is no different than that used by many other practitioners, including Beck and Ellis. Confrontation has been described as holding a mirror up to the client. The style varies, and some confrontation can be harmful (weakness confrontation, which points out a client's weakness), but all addictions treatment approaches include confrontation. Carroll's cognitive-behavioral strategies (structure and format of sessions, client worksheets, samples of confrontations, negotiation of treatment goals) are described in her NIDA manual available online at www.nida.nih.gov/TXManuals/CBT1.html. These excellent concrete strategies will prove useful to counselors.

A counseling approach very similar to the Twelve Step principles is called individualized drug counseling (IDC), developed by Mercer and Woody (1999). Research supports the individualized drug counseling approach, "Patients in IDC reduced their cocaine use more and did so more rapidly than those in the other conditions" (Crits-Christoph et al., 1999). According to the philosophy underlying the individualized drug counseling approach, addiction is a complex disease that damages the addict physically, mentally, and spiritually. The philosophy of this approach incorporates two important elements: endorsement of the disease model and the spiritual dimension of recovery. The disease model essentially states that addiction is more similar to an illness over which one has little, if any, control, than to a behavior one chooses to enact. Recent biologically oriented research suggests a genetic component to alcohol and other addictions, and points to physiological changes in the brain that result from drug use. These findings are very consistent with the disease model (Bloom, 1992; Heinz et al., 1998).

According to Mercer and Woody (1999), spirituality in the individualized drug counseling approach is "very general and not specific to any religion. Three of the main spiritual principles, as taken from Narcotics Anonymous (NA) philosophy, are honesty, openmindedness, and willingness. This spiritual component implies that there is a healing of one's life that needs to take place, and abstinence from the drug is merely the first step rather than the terminal goal." In this approach, recovery involves a return to self-respect through honesty with oneself and others. Spirituality also involves a belief in or sense of connection to something greater than oneself.

The specific drug treated in this description of the approach was cocaine, but it would also apply to any other drug, it would seem. "Addictions counseling" is contrasted with psychotherapy as follows: addictions counseling has short-term goals, behavioral goals, goals directly related to addiction, and it focuses on the present. In contrast, psychotherapy includes short- and long-term goals; cognitive, emotional, and behavioral goals; goals related to all areas of recovery; focus on the past and present. But, as if clear from the description, there is more overlap than not between approaches.

As these authors write, "Addictions Counseling works by first helping the patient recognize the existence of a problem and the associated irrational thinking." Next the patient is encouraged to achieve and maintain abstinence and then to develop necessary psychosocial skills and spiritual development to continue in recovery as a lifelong process. So far the only difference between cognitive-behavioral therapy (CBT) and addictions counseling is the spiritual component. The patient is the agent of change; the patient must take responsibility for developing a program of recovery. "Drug use is thought to be a multidetermined, maladaptive way of coping with life's problems. . . . Compulsive drug abuse is addiction, which is defined as a disease" (Mercer and Woody, 1999).

While these authors contrast individualized drug counseling with cognitive therapy, the strategies are actually a part of cognitive therapy. Cognitive therapy is focused on the present, on concrete options; it can be focused on any specific problem, including drug addiction. The authors state that individualized drug counseling is most similar to the Minnesota Model, also referred to as the Hazelden approach, the CENAPS model (Gorski, 1989), and the Twelve Step facilitation model (Nowinki et al., 1994). The core of these approaches is the same, with individualized drug counseling having the added ingredient of spirituality.

The third and final NIDA manual to be referred to here is a manual for group drug counseling; it is specifically for cocaine but it can be used with other drugs. Group therapy is one of the primary approaches used to treat drug addiction, from inpatient to intensive outpatient to aftercare programs. Results from this study support the idea that a combination of individual and group treatment for cocaine addiction is preferable. The group drug counseling (GDC) model addresses common issues in the early and middle stages of recovery from addiction. The philosophy of the group drug counseling approach is that chemical addictions are complex biopsychosocial diseases that are often chronic and debilitating. Many biological, psychological, sociocultural, and spiritual factors interact to contribute to the development and maintenance of addictions. Research reports show that the combination of individualized drug counseling and group drug counseling produced the best results (Crits-Christoph et al., 1999). Evidence shows that drug abusers need a minimum of three months in outpatient treatment to benefit from treatment (Simpson et al., 1997).

Daley and Mercer (2002) write that group treatment sessions are a vital aspect of recovery from addiction (their manual is available online at www.nida.nih.gov/TXManuals/DCCA/DCCA1.html). In groups clients have the opportunity to learn the facts about addiction and recovery so that they can better understand their drug use problems. Clients also gain strength from each other, learn to use and benefit from social support, and begin to feel valued because they are helping others who are trying to recover.

INTEGRATION
OF APPROACHES

*Adding Motivational Interviewing
to the Cognitive-Behavioral-Twelve Step Mix*

Alluded to above but not introduced is the motivational interviewing approach of William Miller and Stephen Rollnick (1991, 2002). In my first book I described the integration of cognitive behavioral therapy and Twelve Step principles; in this revised edition I am adding motivational interviewing to the mix. According to Liese and Beck (1997) cognitive therapists who treat drug-dependent patients are likely to lose at least 50 percent of their patients to dropout. They suggest that this high dropout rate may be due in part to less than empathic use of cognitive techniques. Their article highlights the importance of timing in using the cognitive behavioral therapy approach. Therapists are encouraged to offer "warm, empathic, collaborative relationships in which drug-dependent patients can feel accepted, understood, and validated." This communication style is best captured in motivational interviewing.

I came upon motivational interviewing only five years ago, while completing a postdoctorate at the Psychiatric Rehabilitation Center at Boston University. Here motivational interviewing was found to work extremely well with people with mental illness and people with the dual disorder of mental illness and substance disorder. Not only is this approach effective in helping the client change; it has the added benefit of preventing counselor burnout. For counselors who find themselves caught up in endless debates and even tirades directed at their clients, motivational interviewing is an essential component to be added to (or to replace) the current tendency to use direct confrontation, also called confrontation-of-denial.

Miller and Rollnick (1991) define motivation and motivational interviewing as follows: "Motivation is a state of readiness or eagerness to change. Motivational interviewing is a confrontational process intended to bring the client to a greater awareness of and personal responsibility for his or her problem and instill commitment to change." They state in the second edition of their book (2002) that while motivational interviewing can be contrasted with different counseling approaches (and they did so in their first edition), this in no way renders motivational interviewing incompatible with other methods. Fundamentally, motivational interviewing is intended to instigate change. They write that, surprisingly, it may not matter if the subsequent treatment is in some way inconsistent with the principles of motivational interviewing. In one study (Miller, 1999), for example, motivational interviewing was given (or not given) at intake in an inpatient treatment program with a confrontive and overly directive approach. Yet program counselors (unaware of group assignment) perceived motivational interviewing clients to be more motivated and compliant in treatment, and twelve-month outcomes were substantially better in the motivational interviewing group than in people who were going through the same inpatient program without motivational interviewing.

In the first edition of their book, they stated that they developed motivational interviewing as a response to the tendency in the addictions field to rely heavily on direct confrontation or confrontation-of-denial. They point out that we need to take into consideration whether the person is ready, willing, and able to change. To begin confronting a client on his need to abstain from substances when this person is not at all interested in that goal is a waste of time and energy. Moreover, whereas counselors once responded to a treatment "failure" by claiming that the client was "not ready" (implying that the client needed to go away, continue to use alcohol or drugs and experience further pain, and then return "ready" for treatment), we now recognize that achieving readiness is part of the therapist's job. As one of my students in recovery said in quoting an anonymous source, "You can lead a horse to water but you can't make him drink ... but you can make him thirsty."

Motivation is viewed as an interpersonal process, the product of an interaction between two people. "Our perspective is that exploring and enhancing motivation for change is itself a proper task, at times even the most important and necessary task, within helping relationships such as counseling, health care, and education" (Miller and Rollnick, 2002).

These authors contrast the motivational approach with the direct confrontation approach that grew from a misinterpretation of A.A. For instance, users of the direct confrontation approach believe that the client must accept the label of alcoholic before change can begin. Insisting that a person label himself an alcoholic can have negative results. I may comply because you are insisting, but secretly I may be saying to myself that it is a lie. I may resist your label, preventing further counselor-client progress. I may leave treatment and return to drugging. Is it not true that I need only recognize that alcohol is a problem in my life in order for me to work on changing that problem? Isn't it also true that in A.A. one need only have the desire to quit in order to attend meetings? Progress, not perfection, is not a slogan only for our addicted clients.

Let's look at some of the essential components of motivational interviewing. The four general principles are: express empathy, develop discrepancy, roll with resistance, and support self-efficacy. Reflective listening or accurate empathy is the key to motivational interviewing. The attitude underlying this principle of empathy is properly termed "acceptance." Note that acceptance is not the same thing as agreement or approval. It is possible to accept and understand a person's perspective while not agreeing with it. Ambivalence (feeling two ways about something, e.g., "I want to quit smoking, but I don't want to give up the pleasure") is accepted as a normal part of human experience and change rather than seen as pathology ("You're a sick person"). So express empathy through acceptance, reflective listening, and recognition that ambivalence is normal.

Motivational interviewing requires some of the same counselor qualities considered essential to client-centered therapy; however, motivational interviewing is not client-centered in the classic sense. Motivational interviewing is intentionally directive — directed toward the resolution of ambivalence. In the first edition of their book, Miller and

Rollnick described motivational interviewing as a confrontational process, and it is. The counselor leads the client to a conclusion about his drinking or drugging: "It creates problems in my life." A second general principle of motivational interviewing is to create and amplify, from the client's perspective, a discrepancy between present behavior and her broader goals or values. When a behavior is seen as conflicting with important personal goals, change is more likely to occur. Discrepancy can be developed by having the client, not the counselor, present the arguments for change; that change is motivated by a perceived discrepancy between present behavior and important personal goals or values.

The third principle is roll with resistance. The counselor does not argue for change while the client is arguing against it. This is counterproductive. "Not only is the ambivalent person unlikely to be persuaded, but direct argument may actually press the person in the opposite direction that he or she is caused to defend" (Miller and Rollnick, 2002). So roll with resistance by avoiding arguments for change, do not directly oppose resistance, invite new perspectives rather than imposing them. The client is the resource for problem solving, and resistance is a signal to respond differently. Addictions counseling is amazingly less stressful when we learn how not to argue with the client.

Support self-efficacy is the fourth principle. Self-efficacy refers to a person's belief that he or she can change, and this belief is an important motivator. The client, not the counselor, is responsible for choosing and carrying out change. The counselor's own belief in the person's ability to change becomes a self-fulfilling prophecy. If we believe our client can change, she is more likely to change; if we believe our client cannot change, she is more likely not to change.

A second key to change in motivational interviewing is taking into consideration the client's stage of change. Stage of change theory was popularized by DiClemente and Prochaska (1985, 1998). We need to recognize the stage of change a person is in and adapt our techniques to that stage. In these stages of change, people progress from precontemplation (not even thinking about it) to maintenance and, perhaps, relapse. Miller and Rollnick (1991) present the following stages and the counselor's motivational tasks that go along with the stage:

Precontemplation is the first state of change, during which the client is "not even thinking about change." If the client is not even thinking about change, we frustrate both the client and ourselves by lecturing him on abstinence. The counselor's motivational task in the precontemplation stage is to "raise doubt" by increasing the client's perception of risks and problems with current behavior. I found this the most critical step toward motivating the client: to find what it is the client values and then help the client to identify the barriers to living that value. For instance, a person with both schizophrenia and marijuana abuse may value independence. Through questioning we discover that the only goal he has is to get his own apartment. What prevents him from getting the apartment is his marijuana use. The motivation to quit smoking marijuana is not because the counselor "says it is bad," but because it is stopping the client from achieving something he values, in this case, independent living.

Contemplation is the next of the stages of change. In this stage the client is both considering and rejecting change; in other words he is ambivalent. He wants to change, but he does not want to deal with the negative consequences of change. The counselor's motivational task is to "tip the balance — evoke reasons to change, risks of not changing; strengthen the client's self-efficacy for change." The decisional balance sheet or pay-off matrix is useful in this stage. Using a matrix, the client fills in the pros and cons of stopping drugs and the pros and cons of continuing to use drugs. For instance, the pros of quitting drugs include better mental and physical health, more money, less trouble with friends, family, the law. The cons of quitting drugs include loss of pleasure in not getting high, increased responsibility, the need to find new friends and a new way of life. The cons of not quitting include continued losses. The pros of not quitting include continued pleasure from getting high and no need to change. We do not pretend that there are no positives associated with using alcohol and drugs. There are; otherwise the person would stop using them. The client needs to develop new beliefs that the negatives outweigh the positives associated with drug use. In addition to tipping the balance toward change, we give the client feedback that she has the strengths needed to make this change.

Determination is the next stage. Determination is the "window of opportunity," during which the client is now more open to change.

According to DiClemente and Prochaska (1998), the counselor's motivational task is to "help the client to determine the best course of action to take in seeking change." The client is presented with choices or options and is responsible for making the choice, the decision. Through problem solving and treatment planning, the counselor presents steps toward achieving the goal.

The *action* stage requires that the person do something about the problem. The counselor helps the client take steps toward change. The next stage, *maintenance*, "requires a different set of skills and strategies." In order to stay in recovery, the client needs to learn how to deal with the realities of life. She may need to learn how to refuse drugs, how to assert herself in a relationship, how to parent, how to apply for and keep a job. A client cannot survive in this new life without new skills. The counselor can help the client develop and use new skills not only to prevent relapse but also to create a new life for herself.

The final stage of change is *relapse,* which is defined by DiClemente and Prochaska as "falling back into old behavior." When this happens the person "needs to restart change." The majority of clients will relapse, and our goal is get them back on track with their recovery. Most addictions counselors will witness an "emotional" or "mental" relapse before the actual relapse into using alcohol or other drugs. Preventing relapse involves identifying these signs and intervening with the client by making her conscious of the behavior and, perhaps, modifying the treatment plan.

Having reviewed the most current and effective strategies, we can move on to see how they can be applied to treating the complicated disease of dual disorder — the co-occurrence of mental illness and substance abuse disorder.

WHAT'S NEW IN TREATMENT POPULATIONS?

Dual Diagnosis

One topic I have added to my addictions counseling course is dual diagnosis: the co-occurrence of substance use disorder and mental illness. Although the concept of "dual disorder" has been around for twenty years, the past decade has seen an increased awareness of the difficulties of treating persons with dual disorder. How do we define dual disorder? The largest body of clinical research in the dual disorder field limits the term "dual disorder" to severe mental illness (SMI) and substance use disorder (S.U.D.) (e.g., Robert Drake and Kim Mueser). Severe mental illness includes only those mental illnesses with psychotic features (e.g., schizophrenia, bipolar disorder, major depression). Other research clinicians include within the "dual disorder" concept not only the less severe Axis I disorders (e.g., transient mood disorders such as depression), but also the Axis II personality disorders such as borderline and antisocial personality disorder (Daley and Moss, 2002).

Optimal treatment is clearly going to depend on the type and severity of the mental illness and of the substance dependence. Treating a person with a dual disorder involving borderline or antisocial personality disorder and one with schizophrenia or severe depression is going to be very different. The overall counseling approach will be similar (cognitive-behavioral-motivational and Twelve Step), but the proportions of the ingredients will vary. In particular, the counselor's confrontive approach needs to vary based on the severity of the mental illness. Further, additional therapies exist that may best deal with specific diagnoses or problems. For instance, the current therapy of choice for borderline disorders appears to be dialectical behavioral therapy, developed by Linehan (1993a, 1993b). This chapter presents the most effective approaches to dual disorder treatment in general. More specific discussion of treatment issues within mental illness types, from personality disorders to schizophrenia, can be found in Daley and Moss (2002). Persons with less severe forms of Axis I mental illness (minor mood disorders, transient adjustment disorders) are not considered to be suffering from "dual disorder."

At one time, the mental health system did not treat people with substance dependence, and the substance dependence system did not treat people with mental health issues — which left the person with dual disorder without adequate treatment. While people with less severe mental illness are now admitted more frequently into substance dependence treatment settings, people with severe mental illness (e.g., bipolar disorder, severe depression, and schizophrenia) are not frequently admitted, or if they are, it is because someone failed to detect the severity of their mental illness. There are some valid reasons for this exclusion. Some addictions treatment settings are not appropriate for people with severe mental illness. For example, a halfway house for persons with addictions is not recommended (Kim Mueser, personal communication, Spring 2000). A halfway house is, by necessity, structured with many rules that the residents must follow. People with severe mental illness would have great difficulty following the many rules, especially if the rules do not have meaning for them. The "house" is an intensive living situation with a lot of people who need to get along and who are required to participate in activities from group to vocational counseling. Often persons with severe mental illness are not able to participate. They sometimes become the scapegoat of the house because they behave differently from other residents. Most importantly, counselors in halfway houses and other addictions settings are frequently not trained as mental health counselors; many of them have minimal training in substance dependence counseling. There are now a limited number of halfway houses solely for persons with dual disorder.

There are differences between the providers of mental health treatment and those of addictions treatment. For many addictions counselors, the only form of confrontation they know is confrontation-of-denial, and this is not effective with the dual disorder population. On the mental health side, training is also lacking. While persons with dual disorder may be admitted to mental health settings, such as supported housing, the mental health counselors frequently do not know how to deal with their substance abuse problems. Often there is no consequence for breaking rules, including the use of alcohol and drugs.

Experts in the dual disorder field, such as Robert Drake, Kim Mueser, and Kenneth Minkoff, believe that progress is being made in the treatment of dual disorder. That may be true from a research perspective, but I do not see it in practice. Ideal treatment programs for persons with dual disorder have been set up for research purposes, but programs available to the general population have not been established. Strides have been made in identifying effective treatment, but there has been little in making this treatment available to more than research participants. The lack of availability of the most effective treatment is a financial and a policy issue. In fact, a few years ago when I was working on a dual disorder book (Doyle Pita and Spaniol, 2002), I was more positive about the increased effectiveness of treatment for dual disorder than I am today. At least in the state of Massachusetts, insurance coverage for the poor is being cut. Treatment settings such as halfway houses had begun accommodating dual disorder persons — at least those with less severe mental disorders. Now they will not because these patients do not have mental health benefits (for psychotherapy or psychoactive medications). Further, due to a lack of funding, practitioners rarely receive the training they need. Although more are being cross-trained now than before, people with dual disorder continue to receive inadequate treatment.

A couple of years ago when I was teaching a dual disorder course at Boston University, a guest speaker whose child has dual disorder was speaking about the impact of dual disorder on the family. She was voicing criticism of the "consumer movement" toward independent living. Her son, now an adult, has the right to independent living, but he continues to use alcohol and attempt suicide when he is living alone. She referred to this as "dying with their rights on." How do we ensure that people with addiction and mental illness enjoy their rights while at the same time protecting them from the negative consequences of these rights and losing them or ourselves in the battle? These are but a few hard questions counselors and family members struggle with in coming to terms with addiction.

In reaction to my lecture on dual disorder, students often question their role in treating people with dual disorder given that they have not received training in mental health. Many of the persons in addictions treatment and many of the persons in mental health treatment have an untreated secondary disorder. In the mental health field, the addictions problem is usually underdiagnosed (Carey and Correia, 1998); in the substance abuse field, the clinicians tend to overdiagnose psychiatric disorders (Delos Reyes, 2002). Being cross-trained in both areas is obviously advantageous for the patient (e.g., he has to keep appointments with one clinician instead of two) and increases the effectiveness of treatment (treating both disorders at once, i.e., integrated treatment, is considered the best treatment). In the absence of cross-training the counselor or clinician needs at least to be able to recognize signs and symptoms and provide the appropriate referral. Further, I encourage consideration of mental illness as more of a continuum than a category. Many of our clients, at least 50 percent we can estimate, will have some type or level of mental illness. Strategies proven effective in treatment of persons with severe mental illness can be useful in treating persons with less severe mental health problems. It may be that our treatment "failures" are people with untreated mental health problems.

The prevalence of coexisting addiction and mental illness is measured from two vantage points: by looking at substance use disorders in persons with mental illness and by looking at psychiatric diagnoses in persons seeking treatment for addiction. To further complicate matters, the prevalence depends also on the particular mental illness, the setting, and the demographics of the population. Persons with severe mental illness who are homeless or in jail or who are assessed in an emergency room or acute care setting are more likely to have substance use disorders than other patients. Substance use disorders tend to be more common in patients who are male, young, single, less educated, and have a family history of substance use disorder. Addiction problems go undetected for a number of reasons. The abuse of alcohol and other drugs occurs in the context of multiple psychosocial dysfunctions due to severe mental illness; therefore the negative consequences of substance abuse may not be as obvious as they would in a person without SMI. The cognitive and emotional effects of substance abuse (depression, anxiety, confusion, hallucinations, delusion) may be misattributed to psychiatric illness. Failure to detect is also due to the patient underreporting his substance use. The patient's denial or minimization may be due to psychological defenses, neuropsychological impairments, lack of insight into connections between drinking and symptoms, or a tendency to provide socially desirable responses. Patients may be motivated to minimize or deny their substance abuse to avoid losing their housing or being discharged from a clubhouse, or any number of other negative consequences. Obviously, these same factors interfere with accurate assessment of persons with substance abuse problems.

Mental health staff may lack the training or expertise to detect substance abuse. Failure to detect substance abuse is likely to lead to inappropriate treatment and poor outcomes (such as relapse). Improved assessment will improve outcome, and new assessment tools are now available to increase the validity of assessment (Rosenberg et al., 1998). In the substance abuse treatment setting, clinicians tend to overdiagnose psychiatric illness; psychiatric disorders are difficult to assess in early recovery because of the acute toxicity of alcohol and other drugs, withdrawal states, and the severe psychosocial stressors associated with addiction. Clinicians need to rely on the history of psychiatric and substance abuse problems, family history, and severity and persistence of symptoms when performing psychiatric assessments.

A generally accepted figure from the mental health setting is that 50 percent to 60 percent of persons with a psychiatric illness also have a substance use problem (Mueser, Drake, and Noordsy, 1998). This high percentage has led experts to state that substance use should be considered the expectation, not the exception (Minkoff, personal communication, Spring 2000). Studies done in addiction treatment settings generally report that 20 percent to 50 percent of patients have one or more psychiatric diagnoses (Delos Reyes, 2002). Major depression is common in those with alcoholism and opioid dependence. Bipolar disorders are often seen in those with cocaine dependence and alcoholism. Mood disorders include depressive disorders and bipolar disorders. Treatment obstacles include denial of the secondary disorder. For instance, a patient with comorbid depression and addiction may deny one or both of these disorders. The patient may feel that she is not really an addict after all ("I only drank because I was depressed") and only has to take antidepressant medications without working a program of recovery. On the other hand, she may reject treatment of depression and rely only addiction treatment for her mental health ("When I'm sober, I will no longer feel depressed"). Denial of either illness can lead to relapse; clinicians must consistently reinforce that the patient has two chronic conditions, each requiring different types of treatment. So, in sum, we as counselors or clinicians must first assess the coexisting disorders, and then we must help the patient accept the diagnoses and treatment. Best treatment for depression, for example, is a combination of education, psychotherapy (relapse prevention, preparing patient for Twelve Step participation), and medication (Delos Reyes, 2002).

When discussing dual disorder one cannot escape either the "chicken and egg" or "self-medication" arguments. That is, does one drug because one has a mental illness or does one have a mental illness because one drugs? Don't practically all alcoholics and drug addicts use substances to alter their feelings, to "self-medicate"? Daley and Moss (2002) outline the possible interactions between chemical dependency and psychiatric disorders, paraphrased as follows: chemical dependency increases the risk of developing a psychiatric illness; psychiatric illness increases the risk of chemical dependency; psychiatric symptoms may affect the onset, duration, or response to treatment of chemical dependency; chemical dependency affects adherence to psychiatric treatment and clinical outcome. Further, psychiatric symptoms may arise as a direct result of chronic substance abuse or withdrawal. For example, users of PCP or stimulants may become psychotic and resemble schizophrenics. Symptoms of psychiatric illness may result as the indirect consequences of chemical dependency, e.g., trouble at work or legal problems. Over time, the symptoms of chemical dependency and psychiatric illness may become linked, making it difficult to determine which is primary and which is secondary. Finally, the dual disorders can develop independently, that is, with one not being the cause of the other. We can attempt to determine which came first by taking a thorough history or by putting the person on a "drug vacation" for several months to see which, if any, psychiatric symptoms remain. No matter what the interaction between the illnesses, where two illnesses exist, both must be addressed and addressed at the same time.

Ideally a person with dual disorder will be treated in an integrated treatment program, which can be defined as one in which the same clinician (or team of clinicians) provides treatment for both mental illness and the substance use disorder at the same time. The essential components of integrated treatment are assertive outreach, comprehensiveness, shared decision making, long-term commitment, stage-wise treatment, and pharmacotherapy (Mueser, Drake, and Noordsy, 1998). Kim Mueser is arguably the most prominent of research practitioners in the field of dual diagnosis.

Assertive outreach refers to providing services in patients' natural environment rather than only in the clinic. Assertive outreach has become a component of substance abuse treatment, e.g., when an outreach worker goes to the streets to educate and assist the addict.

Comprehensiveness reinforces the idea that a person not only must stop using substances but also must learn to lead an abstinent life. Persons with dual diagnosis have a wide range of needs, such as improving the quality of their family and social relationships, and managing anxiety and depression. Those already working in the field, especially in a residential setting, may recognize that a wide range of needs is also characteristic of many clients with substance abuse. A person using substances across a lifetime has not learned how to function in roles and has not learned how to identify and cope with feelings. As Mueser, Drake, and Noordsy (1998) write:

> The recovery process takes years, not days or months. Every stage of treatment involves a comprehensive approach. Clients make progress even before they acknowledge their substance abuse or develop motivation to reduce alcohol and drug use by improving their skills and supports. These improvements will increase their hopefulness about making positive changes and will facilitate their subsequent efforts to attain abstinence. As they attempt to live their lives without alcohol and drugs, they must be able to handle distress, to find meaningful activities, to have a constructive social network including rewarding friendships, and to live in a safe setting. Otherwise, they are very unlikely to maintain abstinence.

Comprehensiveness also reinforces the value of stage theory; even in the precontemplative stage the person is making progress. This allowance of reduced harm rather than insisting on abstinence of substances has become more popular over the last decade as we have begun to recognize that clients or patients are not always, or even usually, going to do it "our way." In harm reduction the goal is to reduce the harm associated with substance use rather than completely quitting use of the substance. Clean needles exchange programs and methadone therapy can be viewed as harm reduction strategies for heroin addicts.

Shared decision making recognizes that persons with dual disorder are capable of playing a critical role in the management of their disorders and in making progress toward achieving their goals. Shared decision making also recognizes the critical role that many families play in the lives of persons with severe mental illness. Since they are often involved as caregivers and serve to buffer patients from many of the negative effects of stress, families also need to be engaged and involved in making decisions. In addictions, we rarely hear about family involvement unless the client is a child or adolescent. This is a difference between the mental health field and the addictions field. The mental health providers tend to play more of a caretaker role than does the substance abuse treatment provider. The mental health provider is more likely to be seen as guilty of enabling the person with mental illness. Enabling in this case is defined as a negative behavior that allows the client or patient to not take responsibility for his life, to continue to act in ways that have negative consequences (such as spending all his money, engaging in risky sexual behavior, or smoking marijuana). Similarly, the family of the person with mental illness is also more likely to take the caretaker role. We will revisit the role of the family when we reach the section on family therapy.

It is more difficult to draw the line with persons with dual disorder because it is difficult to determine what they are — and are not — capable of doing. We would expect a substance abuser to be able at some point to obtain and keep employment. We would therefore expect her to become financially responsible. What about the person with dual disorder? Persons with severe mental illness have difficulty keeping a job once they have it. They continue to be financially dependent on their families and the families continue to oversee in some respects the person's life because financial resources affect almost all of life. How can one support a family without financial resources? The inability to function in life roles (even though one is sober) is perhaps a red flag indicating mental illness. Persons with severe mental illness lack role functions; persons with mental illness will demonstrate behavior that interferes with role functioning. If we can engage a person in treatment by providing her with rewards (food and clothing) despite her continued use, are you enabling her? Or is this harm reduction?

Stage-wise treatment is a concept introduced earlier in the section on motivational interviewing. The stages of change discussed earlier differ somewhat from the stages in this section; however, the point is the same: changes occur in a series of stages. Recognizing stages of treatment helps the clinician to choose which interventions are most likely to be successful at a particular point of recovery. Four stages of recovery are described: engagement, persuasion, active treatment, and relapse prevention (Osher and Kofoed, 1989). Mueser uses these stages in his work with persons with dual disorder, and what follows is a description of how he applies these stages in his work.

Mueser defines engagement by the absence of a working alliance between the patient and the clinician. "Because the clinician cannot help the patient modify her substance use behavior without a therapeutic relationship, the goal of the engagement stage is to establish such an alliance, defined as meeting on a regular (at least weekly) basis" (Mueser, Drake, and Noordsy, 1998). Clinical interventions for the engagement stage involve practical assistance with securing food, clothing, and shelter, crisis intervention, and support. In working with dual disorder clients, as in working with unmotivated clients, the goal is to identify what it is they value. They may value obtaining food or clothing. Providing them with the means of obtaining what it is *they* value will reinforce their continued involvement in therapy and, hopefully, progress toward the next stage.

The persuasion stage parallels the contemplative phase in the stages of change model. The client is thinking about quitting his use of substances, but he doesn't want to deal with the negative consequences. He is ambivalent: "I want to quit smoking, but I would miss hanging out with my friends who smoke." Patients who are behaviorally unmotivated are in the persuasion stage. The goals are the same: help the patient recognize that substance use is a problem, develop hopefulness that life can be improved by reducing substance use, and demonstrate motivation by attempting to change behavior. In this phase, active psychiatric symptoms are stabilized at the same time as the patient receives substance abuse counseling to minimize the interference from grandiosity, psychosis, or thought disorder. Individual and family education regarding psychiatric illness and substance abuse are provided. Motivational interviewing is used to help the client identify his own goals and to discover how substance use interferes with the achievement of those goals. Group interventions and persuasion groups provide the patient the opportunity to discuss with peers the pros and cons of substance abuse. Safe "damp" or "wet" housing tolerates a certain amount of substance abuse — e.g., use may be permitted outside of the house but not in the house. Medications to treat psychiatric illness may have a secondary effect on craving or addiction. Family interventions and recreational and social activities are also used during persuasion.

The active treatment stage does not occur until the person has changed behaviors by significantly reducing substance use and is actively seeking to sustain or enhance reduction. The goal of this stage is to help the patient reduce substance use to the point of eliminating negative consequences or to attain abstinence for a prolonged period. This goal is the same as that of harm reduction. The strategies of active treatment in dual disorder are very similar to those used with substance abusers. Clinical strategies may include family problem solving, peer groups, social skills training to help deal with risky situations, self-help groups (e.g., A.A.), individual cognitive-behavioral counseling, pharmacological treatments to support abstinence (e.g., disulfiram, naltrexone), safe housing, detoxification, and contingency management (such as monetary reinforcement for not using substances).

The relapse prevention stage is reached when the person has not experienced negative consequences related to substance use (or has been abstinent) for at least six months. The overarching goal of this stage is to develop a meaningful recovery. Clinicians facilitate a shift in focus from giving up substances to gaining a healthy life. Interventions include supported or independent employment, involvement in peer groups and self-help groups, social skills training, family problem solving, lifestyle improvements (e.g., smoking cessation, healthy diet, regular exercise), and independent housing.

The whole person must be addressed in each stage of recovery, and this requires a combination of therapies from cognitive to motivational to self-help involvement to pharmacotherapy. When treating substance abusing clients we need to keep in mind the necessity of involving many such clinical interventions.

= T E N =

SPECIAL TOPICS IN ADDICTION

Nicotine, Medication, Family,
Women, and Adolescents

Nicotine Dependence

I am starting off this chapter with nicotine dependence as a symbolic gesture because nicotine dependence is typically the last issue to be addressed. Nicotine dependence is one of the most critical issues and, at the same time, the least likely to be viewed as a treatment issue in the addictions treatment field by everyone—from administrators to direct care counselors. First some facts.

More than four hundred thousand people in the United States die every year from tobacco-related illnesses. This represents more deaths than those caused by the *combination* of alcohol, cocaine, heroin, AIDS, suicides, homicides, fires, airplane and car crashes, and the death penalty. More than 90 percent of those who begin smoking become addicted. Nicotine is a high potency alkaloid with a short half-life that releases dopamine, growth hormone, and cortisol into the central nervous system, with stimulant effects similar to amphetamines and cocaine. Nicotine withdrawal is characterized by symptoms of irritability, anxiety, bradycardia, insomnia, hunger, and difficulty concentrating. Even one day without smoking causes significant increases in response time on a rapid arithmetic test (Delos Reyes, 2002).

Treatment of nicotine dependence is difficult but obviously worth the effort to eliminate the pain and suffering caused by its use. Clinicians can begin by assessment of the patient's "stage of change." According to Rustin (2002), patients in the preparation (or determination) stage should use a "quit date," which is usually two or more weeks in the future. The patient should be the one to select the date and the date should have meaning to the person (e.g., birthday, New Year's Day). The counselor and client together develop a plan for abstinence for the quit date. For those in the contemplation stage, completing a decisional analysis matrix (listing pros and cons of quitting and not quitting) is also useful in tipping the balance to quitting.

As counselors we need to educate ourselves on the effective methods of treatment, including use of medications. The two medications for nicotine replacement are nicotine replacement therapy (NRT) and buprion (an antidepressant). Both treat nicotine withdrawal, but only buprion reduces craving. Combining both medications results in a higher quit rate than either medication alone. Medication doubles the success rate in smoking cessation, although 85 percent of the people who have quit smoking have not used medication (Delos Reyes, 2002).

Given that we are aware of the deadly consequences of smoking and we know what works in smoking cessation, why do so many clients continue to smoke? There continues to be a high level of ambivalence connected to the whole smoking issue. Many addictions and mental health counselors themselves continue to smoke. Although intellectually recognizing that cigarette smoking is an addiction, they continue to deny that it is the same as other drugs of abuse. In many facilities, counselors continue to smoke *with* their clients, yes, *with* their clients. This is not limited to addictions settings; it is also a common occurrence in mental health settings. Currently, I am teaching a class where nearly all the students work in supported housing with dual disorder residents. Counselors smoking with their clients is considered therapeutic, the idea being that it is a way to bond with the client. Unfortunately, while we are "bonding" with the client, we are reinforcing her smoking and enabling her to die of a tobacco-related illness. Further, this student said that counselors who smoked were viewed more favorably and responded to more positively by the clients. Thus, not only is the counselor's smoking reinforcing client smoking; client smoking is reinforcing the counselor's smoking. We need to find healthier ways to bond or be empathic with our clients.

While I was working in a halfway house, the Department of Public Health made available *free of charge* nicotine dependence treatment, even coming out to the site to provide treatment. Approximately one-fourth of the residents and staff signed up for it, and maybe one-tenth attended one-quarter of the sessions. The staff did not take seriously and did not support smoking cessation. Moreover, they continued to smoke with the residents. The program was doomed to failure.

As an ex-smoker, I can attest to the difficulty of quitting. But that is true of all addictions and all negative behaviors. We cannot continue to excuse smoking behavior simply because we have not gotten a handle on it ourselves. Counselors and clients sharing an addictive behavior in addiction and mental health settings has to stop. Like it or not, counselors are perceived by clients as role models. Counselors need to take seriously and promote smoking cessation. In the very least, counselors need to stop allowing their addiction to negatively affect the lives of those they are paid to help.

Medication

A book on addictions counseling would not be complete without a section on medications, given the increasing use of medications with persons who are substance dependent. Two groups of medications are of interest here. There are medications prescribed for chemical dependency and psychiatric medications prescribed for patients who appear to have the symptoms of various mental disorders. There are pros and cons to every prescribed medication. First, the positives.

Drug Addiction Treatment Medications

Medications are most effective when combined with counseling. Medication treatments are currently available for opiate dependence, post-detoxification craving for alcohol, and nicotine dependence. There are currently no medications approved by the Food and Drug Administration for treating addiction to cocaine, LSD, PCP, marijuana, methamphetamine and other stimulants, inhalants, or anabolic steroids. There are medications, however, for treating the adverse health effects of these drugs, such as seizure and psychotic reactions, and for overdoses from opiates. Currently, NIDA's top research priority is the development of a medication useful in treating cocaine addiction.

The primary medically assisted withdrawal method for narcotic addiction is to switch the patient to a comparable drug that produces milder withdrawal symptoms and then gradually taper off the substitute medication. The medication used most often is methadone, taken by mouth once a day. Patients are started on the lowest dose that prevents the more severe signs of withdrawal, and then the dose is gradually reduced. Once a patient goes through withdrawal, there is still considerable risk of relapse. Patients may return to taking drugs even though they no longer have physical withdrawal symptoms. A great deal of research is being done to find medications that can block drug craving and treat other factors that cause a return to drugs. Patients who cannot continue abstaining from opiates are given maintenance therapy, usually methadone. The maintenance doses of methadone prevent both withdrawal symptoms and heroin craving. They also prevent addicts from getting a high from heroin and, as a result, they stop using it. Research has shown that maintenance therapy reduces the spread of AIDS in the treated population. The overall death rate is also significantly reduced.

Of the various methadone programs, those that provide higher doses of methadone have better retention rates. Also, those that provide other services, such as counseling, therapy, and medical care, along with methadone get better results.

Those are the positives associated with drug addiction medications such as methadone, but there are negatives as well. Methadone treatment continues to be highly controversial among addictions counselors and those in recovery from addictions. A major problem lies in the methadone clinics themselves. There are not enough quality adjunct services being offered (such as counseling). There is not enough quality control or oversight by watchdog agencies. The clients at these agencies are too many and the services too few. Clients' blood levels are not checked adequately, many addicts "on the program" are getting doses that are too high, many are using methadone in combination with other illicit drugs, and others are selling their methadone on the street. There is a move away from daily dosing to cut costs. Increasingly, addicts are given more than one dose to take home; there is even discussion of a thirty-pak to take home, increasing the likelihood of abuse and over-dose. Addicts can still get a "high" from the methadone if the dose is too high. Many question the quality of life of being "on the program." Many do not think that a person on methadone is "in recovery." Many do not think that people on the program should be allowed in treatment settings such as halfway houses because of the effect on the other residents. They believe it can be a trigger for other addicts trying to remain abstinent. Methadone clinic operators are criticized for being motivated by money and, therefore, not motivated to encourage addicts to get off methadone. There is not enough research on the long-term side effects of methadone; there is not enough research on the interaction of methadone with other medications such as psychiatric medications taken by dual disorder patients. These are a few of the many issues debated around methadone use.

In response to questions such as these with regard to methadone, in October 2002 buprenorphine, a new drug for treating opioid abuse, was approved by the U.S. Food and Drug Administration (*NIDA Notes*, November 2002). Currently, only one-fifth of the estimated heroin addicts are being treated at methadone clinics. This will be the first medication for opioid maintenance treatment that physicians can dispense in their offices to patients addicted to heroin and prescription pain relievers. According to research reports, unlike methadone, this drug has a low potential for diversion to illicit use because it produces less stimulation and physical dependence. It blocks heroin's effects, reduces craving for the drug, and prevents withdrawal symptoms. The hope is that office-based treatment with buprenorphine will provide a treatment option for the eight hundred thousand opiate-addicted individuals not now being treated. Only time will tell how effective this treatment is in helping opioid abusers into recovery.

Psychiatric Medication

The second group of medications of interest is those used to treat psychiatric symptoms. Few would argue that persons with severe mental illness do not need psychiatric medications. There are still those who say that persons on psychiatric medications are not abstinent and therefore not in recovery; however, these people are fewer in number.

Perhaps the greatest problems are created by the prescription of psychiatric medication for those who do not have a severe mental disorder but who exhibit lesser symptoms of, say, depression and anxiety. Too often psychiatric medications are overprescribed as a quick fix and in place of psychotherapy or counseling. It is cheaper to meet with a patient for fifteen to twenty minutes and write her a prescription than it is to provide fifty minutes of psychotherapy or counseling and encourage her on the road to recovery.

Too often the patient simply switches her dependency from one drug to another. Many clients know of a doctor in their area who will hand out whatever drugs they ask for, or they will find several doctors — getting prescriptions from their primary physician, psychiatrist, pain specialist, and even their dentists. I have known dentists to prescribe the highly addictive Oxycontin to women who are currently living in a halfway house attempting to recover from their addictions. Others begin their addiction with a prescription, especially with the highly addictive pain medications prescribed for chronic pain. The patient reasons that the doctor must know what she is doing. Unfortunately, sometimes she does not. If the patient took the medication as prescribed, it would not pose a problem. But when a doctor prescribes addictive medication to an addict, there is the likelihood that the addict will abuse the medication.

Clinicians know that prescribing some medications to patients will reduce their emotional upset, their anxiety or depression. But if their anxiety or depression is reality-based (e.g., in response to living in an abusive relationship), then the drug can allow the person to tolerate the situation. That is not a positive outcome. All drugs have side effects. We must weigh the pros and cons of prescribing every medication. Clearly, professionals need to increase their awareness of the potential negative psychological and physical side effects when prescribing medications.

When it comes to persons with dual disorder with severe mental illness, we have a new set of problems, especially involving compliance since patients frequently do not take the medication prescribed. For instance, the rate of medication noncompliance among outpatients with schizophrenia has been reported to be as high as 50 percent. "In the clinical setting, the patient's acceptance or rejection of prescribed pharmacological regimens is often the single greatest determinant of the treatments' effectiveness" (Fenton, Blyler, and Heinssen, 1997). Compliance is affected by many factors. Patient-related factors include increased severity of symptoms or grandiosity or both, lack of insight, and substance abuse. Medication-related factors include unpleasant side effects and dosage problems (too high, too low). Environmental factors include inadequate support or supervision and practical barriers such as lack of money or transportation. Clinician-related factors include poor therapeutic alliance.

A major negative side effect of psychiatric medications is their potential for abuse. NIDA presents the following data regarding prescription drug abuse, by type of prescription, by age, and by gender. Knowing who is at increased risk will help in the detection and prevention of prescription drug abuse. In 1999, an estimated 4 million people, about 2 percent of the population age twelve and older, were currently (within the past month) using prescription drugs nonmedically. Of these, 2.6 million misused pain relievers, 1.3 million misused sedatives and tranquilizers, and 0.9 million misused stimulants. While prescription drug abuse affects many Americans, some trends of particular concern are seen among elders, adolescents, and women.

The misuse of prescribed mediations may be the most common form of drug abuse among the elderly. Older people are prescribed medications about three times more frequently than the general population and have poorer compliance with directions for use.

The National Household Survey on Drug Abuse numbers indicate that the sharpest increases in new users of prescription drugs for nonmedical purposes occur in twelve to seventeen and eighteen to twenty-five year olds. Among twelve to fourteen year olds, psychotherapeutics (e.g., pain killers, tranquilizers, sedatives, and stimulants) were reported to be one of two primary drugs used.

Overall, men and women have similar rates of nonmedical use of prescription drugs, with the exception of twelve to seventeen year olds. In this age group, young women are more likely than young men to use psychotherapeutic drugs nonmedically. Also, among women and men who use either a sedative, an anti-anxiety drug, or a hypnotic, women are almost twice as likely to become addicted.

The most commonly abused drugs belong to three classes: opioids (often prescribed to treat pain), central nervous system depressants (used to treat anxiety and sleep disorders), and stimulants (prescribed to treat narcolepsy and attention deficit/hyperactivity disorder). As addictions or dual disorder counselors, can we do anything to increase medication compliance? We can work to decrease substance abuse. We can take a history of the client's medication and compliance, and consequent effects of noncompliance. We can continue to educate the client about the need for medication compliance. We can discuss the consequence of noncompliance for the therapeutic relationship; for instance in some treatment settings compliance is a condition of continued treatment. As with treatment adherence in general, we can increase our attention to the therapeutic alliance. We can improve the therapeutic relationship by shifting to motivational interviewing strategies (empathy, decisional balancing, negotiating goals). We may need to renegotiate treatment goals. For instance, the client's goals may be to maintain sexual functioning, to avoid obesity, and not to miss work for doctor's appointments. The provider's primary goal may be relapse prevention. We need to understand the causes of noncompliance and then develop a plan of intervention with the client.

Family Treatment

Family treatment is particularly important in helping elders, women, and children recover. There are many issues relevant to the impact of family and significant others on the client. The patient might be the adult in the family (parent or spouse) or the child in the family (either a child by age or an adult child still dependent on the family). When it is the adult in the family with the substance abuse problem, typically family treatment is limited. The family or some family members may attend "family treatment" meetings, which are an adjunct to the substance abuse treatment (e.g., they may attend a two- or three-day family session, either individually or in a group). Alternatively, the patient may be a child or adolescent being treated for substance abuse, and the parents, and sometimes the rest of the family, are involved in family treatment. Again, the family treatment is typically an adjunct to the substance abuse treatment. Family sessions are helpful in teaching the other family members about the disease of addiction and how to deal with their addicted or their newly sober family member.

There is more family involvement when a family member is mentally ill or has dual disorder (both mental illness and substance abuse). This is due in part to the different views taken of mental illness and substance dependence, with family members and significant others more likely to view substance use as a choice. In fact, both substance dependence and mental illness are diseases, and the processes very similar. Both require vigilance and maintenance on the part of the patient to manage the symptoms. The person with psychotic symptoms must take his medication to prevent relapse; the person with drug addiction must attend treatment and follow the steps recommended to prevent relapse. Likewise, the person with mental illness is just as likely to have her negative behaviors enabled as is the person with substance dependence, but usually for different reasons.

The person with mental illness is too often perceived as not capable of responsible behavior and therefore is "taken care of" by others. The addict is often enabled through more subtle family dynamics. For instance, untreated family members may find rewards in having a family member actively drinking or drugging. The spouse or parent may be the patient's drinking or drugging "buddy." I am finding of late that often the parent has introduced the child to drugs and continues to drug and drink with the child. Other family members are accustomed to the patient being the "sick one" in the family and blaming her for all that goes wrong in the family. Once this family member is not "to blame," then the other members need to start looking at themselves, which is not a comfortable position for many. For instance, having an addicted child in the house might keep a couple together fighting for a common cause and keeping the focus off troubles in their marriage. A parent who is divorced or single may rail against the substance use of her adult child but also reinforce that behavior in order to prevent him from getting sober and moving on.

As treatment providers we are interested in changing the dynamics of the family system that reinforces or enables the negative behavior (drinking, drugging, lying, stealing, harming other family members verbally or physically, and so forth). The most frequent reason for return to old behaviors is that the family sets limits or boundaries and then moves them once the person breaks the agreement. For instance, living at home may be conditional on the person not drinking or drugging. But will the family be able to throw the person out if she breaks the rule? Often the person is allowed to stay and is subjected to the anger and threats of the family members; this does not promote abstinence. The person is repeatedly given "one last chance," and this one last chance inevitably becomes another and another until the addicted person requires another stay in detox or dies from medical consequences. The family members must set appropriate limits and back them up. Family members affected by the behavior of the addict may find help in individual counseling or self-help meetings such as Al-Anon or Co-Dependents Anonymous.

Family members and other significant others are not the only enablers in the life of the mentally ill or substance dependent person; program staff also enable negative behavior. In supported housing of the mentally ill person, the staff may excuse negative behavior or look the other way when it occurs. This is due in part to the perceived helplessness of the patient, but it also is due to patient rights, program policies, and a simple lack of staff to attend to problems. Persons with dual disorder living independently in supported housing have the freedom to drink alcohol, even if they are alcoholic. There may be consequences only when drinking alcohol interferes with the person's fulfillment of other obligations, such as paying the rent, so the reaction to alcohol use is not immediate. Even when the person is discovered using illicit drugs, such as marijuana, the reaction is often nonconfrontive and slow in coming. In contrast, if this person is in substance abuse treatment, e.g., a recovery home, he is subject to random toxicology screens and immediately discharged if he tests positive for use of any chemicals, regardless of whether he has a coexisting disorder.

The most productive response is somewhere in the middle of this continuum from "doing nothing" to "throwing them out." There must always be an immediate negative response as a consequence of drinking or drugging. Expression of disappointment or anger is typically not effective in stopping negative behavior. The consequence must be the loss of something that the person values, usually a loss of privilege. Motivational interviewing techniques outlined by Miller and Rollnick (2002) are extremely helpful in this regard, as are techniques outlined by Mueser and Fox (1998) for families dealing with severe mental illness and substance use disorders.

As Daley and Mercer (2002) write, "There is an association between relapse and social supports across a range of addictions. Involving the family or significant other of the addicted client in individual or multiple family group sessions can reduce the risk of relapse." Their group drug counseling (GDC) model includes a one-time family psychoeducational workshop conducted during the first month of treatment. Similar workshops have been used with all types of psychiatric and addictive disorders. The positive impacts on the family include lessening the family burden, increasing helpful behaviors, and decreasing unhelpful behaviors. Some of the specific benefits include providing the counseling staff with an opportunity to learn about the client's family, observing how family members interact and gaining input from the family; facilitating compliance with treatment; providing family members the opportunity to voice their concerns and feelings; and allowing the client to hear how the family experiences the addiction.

Daley and Mercer's family psychoeducational workshop is limited in time and scope due to the setting and fact that it is research-based. These authors state that in community-based programs, a variety of family approaches are recommended, including multiple family groups, family psychoeducational workshops, individual family sessions, sessions with individual family members based on a specific need, and referral to family-related self-help programs.

Women and Addiction

Are there gender differences in addiction? The research shows many differences. Data from a year 2000 survey by the Substance Abuse and Mental Health Services Administration (SAMHSA) shows that women tend to have lower rates of past-month use of alcohol, tobacco, and other drugs than men. This difference disappears in youths (age twelve to seventeen), with females having higher rates of cigarette smoking and similar rates of alcohol consumption and illicit drug use as compared with males. Gender differences in substance abuse can be divided into several categories: social issues, psychiatric problems, differences in biological response, and medical consequences.

Women experience more social disapproval if they use alcohol and other drugs. Women with alcoholism are more likely to have alcoholic spouses and alcoholic role models in their families of origin. Research shows that up to 70 percent of drug abusing women report histories of physical and sexual abuse (NIDA Infofax, 2000). More women than men are divorced. This is probably due to the disruption in family life caused by substance abuse; men experience more disruption in employment.

Women tend to have psychiatric problems before experiencing substance use disorders; men show the opposite pattern. Women alcoholics have higher rates of depression, panic disorder, and phobias than male alcoholics. Men with substance use disorders are more than twice as likely to be diagnosed with conduct disorder and antisocial personality disorders. For women, depression is more associated with relapse after treatment, and depressed women are less successful than depressed men in smoking cessation. Men and women alcoholics have similar rates of illicit drug use.

With regard to biological differences, women metabolize nicotine more slowly then men. Women have less gastric alcohol dehydrogenase, causing higher levels of intoxication after drinking smaller amounts than men. More alcoholic women than men die from cirrhosis. Some studies suggest that progression is faster in women than men.

Pregnant women generally use alcohol, tobacco, and marijuana at about half the rates of nonpregnant women, with the exception of pregnant adolescents (age fifteen to seventeen years) who use at about the same rate as nonpregnant adolescents. Pregnant women who use drugs and alcohol are at a higher risk for conception delay, infertility, ectopic pregnancy, spontaneous abortion, preterm delivery, lower birth weight babies, and fetal alcohol syndrome.

In terms of treatment, women represent one-third of all treatment admissions. Women are more likely to be treated for "hard" drugs such as cocaine and heroin. The criminal justice system tends to refer more men than women to treatment (39 percent versus 25 percent), while women addicts are more likely to seek treatment in a health care setting or some other nonsubstance use setting. Once in treatment, women tend to do as well as men.

Many women who use drugs lack self-confidence, have low self-esteem, and feel powerless. Many do not seek treatment because they are afraid. Treatment barriers include child care and child custody issues. Women fear not being able to take care of or keep their children, they fear reprisal from their spouses and boyfriends, and they fear punishment from authorities in the community. Often their drug-using male partners initiated them into drug abuse, and many have difficulty abstaining from drugs when their male partner supports their use.

Research shows that women benefit the most from drug treatment programs that provide a wide range of services, including the following: food, clothing, shelter, transportation, job counseling and training, legal assistance, literacy training, family therapy, couples counseling, medical care, child care, social support, psychological assessment and mental health care, and family planning. Research also shows that for women, in particular, a continuing relationship with a treatment provider is an important factor throughout treatment.

Anecdotal information gained through my experience and conversation with other therapists and counselors suggests that women are more complicated than men to treat. For women who have children, care of their children is at the forefront of treatment. Soon after they enter treatment, they begin to shift the focus from themselves to their children. This brings up feelings of guilt about not being a good parent and feelings of anger at self and others (such as the legal system, parents, and especially the fathers of the children). While men are also faced with parenting issues in treatment, they are rarely as immediate. That is, the woman is typically the primary caregiver. The woman is faced immediately with having to cope with the children, initially on a time-limited basis during visits but on a 24/7 basis after discharge. The woman in recovery has to plan not only for the care of herself but for the care of her children. She has to organize herself (meetings, appointments, job training, etc.) around the life of the children (child care, school, appointments, etc.).

On top of the demands or organizing around child care is the problem of arranging visits with the father of the children. Often the woman no longer has a relationship with the father, and the father may be in a treatment facility or prison. Visits with children and the father of the children, while necessary and often with a positive outcome, are triggers to relapse. A woman in early recovery has not learned how to cope with the intense feelings brought on by this contact. Some have lost custody to the father. The father may have been abusive to her and the children. Now if she wants to see her children, the woman is forced to go to court to request contact. Often she feels the children were unfairly taken away (even if as she admits to blackouts while the children were under her care). Often the father was as unhealthy as she at the time; often he is still an addict but has the financial ability to keep her from the children. On the other side of the coin, men in treatment also complain about unfair treatment by the courts, with the courts limiting their contact or issuing a restraining order based on the say-so of the spouse or girlfriend.

We have seen many women rush to get back their children only to quickly relapse once they have them. Bad for the children, bad for the women. The best we can do in treatment is provide as much support as possible and recommend limited contact or responsibility for care until the woman is strong enough to manage these painful feelings. While there may be complicating factors for women, the process and techniques of counseling are essentially the same for men and women. We can help women identify their needs, prioritize issues, and challenge faulty beliefs regarding their children and the abuse they have suffered at the hands of their parents and significant others.

Adolescents and Addiction

Many factors influence adolescent drug abuse. Peer relationships; family, school, and neighborhood environments; and social or cultural norms can each act as protective factors or can increase risk. This section takes a look at the trends and treatment of adolescent treatment.

Adolescent drug use is actually on the decline, according to most recent research reports (NIDA Infofax, 2002). Since 1975, the Monitoring The Future (MTF) project has annually studied the extent of drug abuse among high school twelfth graders. This survey was expanded in 1991 to include eighth and tenth graders.

The 2002 MTF study marks the sixth year in a row that illicit drug use among eighth, tenth, and twelfth graders remained stable or decreased. In particular, the proportion of eighth and tenth graders reporting the use of any illicit drug in the prior twelve months declined significantly from 2001 to 2002. The decrease in illicit drug use among eighth graders continues a decline begun in 1997, but this is the first significant decline since 1998. Specific decreases were noted in the use of marijuana, some club drugs, cigarettes, and alcohol. In addition, MDMA (Ecstasy) also decreased in all three grades. LSD showed their lowest rates in history. For alcohol, the use rates for eighth and tenth graders are at record lows in the history of the survey. Use of anabolic, androgenic steroids remained stable from 2001 to 2002. Use of amphetamines is down significantly for eighth graders. Nonmedical use of methylphenidate (Ritalin) was stable.

For the first time, in 2002 the MTF survey looked at the misuse of Oxycontin and Vicodin. Nonmedical use of Oxycontin in the past year was reported by 4 percent of twelfth graders, and Vicodin use in the same time period was reported by 9.6 percent of twelfth graders. The only significant increases in drug use in the 2002 survey were past-year crack use by tenth graders, up from 1.8 to 2.3 percent, and past-year sedative use by twelfth graders, from 5.9 percent in 2001 to 7 percent in 2002.

How much of the most frequently abused drugs are they using? For cigarettes, past-month use figures are:

eighth grade: 12.2 percent in 2001 to 10.7 percent in 2002
tenth grade: 21.3 percent to 17.7 percent
twelfth grade: 29.5 percent to 26.7 percent

Daily use in past month:

tenth grade: 12.2 percent in 2001 to 10.1 percent in 2002
twelfth grade: 19.0 percent to 16.9 percent

For marijuana/hashish, among tenth graders, use in the past year decreased from 32.7 percent in 2001 to 30.3 percent in 2002; past-month use decreased from 19.8 percent to 17.8 percent; and daily use in the past month decreased from 4.5 percent to 3.9 percent.

While it is positive to note the decline in use across most drugs, the amount used, particularly of marijuana, and especially by young children, is alarming. In 1999, more than 2 million Americans used marijuana for the first time. Two-thirds of them were between the ages of twelve and seventeen. Furthermore, the marijuana that is available today can be five times more potent than the marijuana of the 1970s. One author writes of the years 2000 and 2002 marijuana data: "More and more young Americans are using cannabis. Initial cannabis use is starting at progressively younger ages; nearly one-fourth of eighth graders have used cannabis." Howell (2002) writes that "cannabis use is now at an all-time peak in Americans twelve to eighteen years of age, with nearly half of the high school seniors reporting lifetime use and nearly one-fourth reporting use in the past month."

I find marijuana abuse particularly difficult to treat because the users are especially resistant to recognizing the negative consequences of use — other than the fact that it is illegal and you can be arrested. The negative consequences of marijuana, like those of cigarettes, are not as immediate as those of other drugs. I have not treated anyone for cannabis dependence who has come without coercion (from the legal system, school, or parents), whether adolescent or adult. Contrary to popular belief, marijuana can be addictive. Marijuana can produce adverse physical, mental, emotional, and behavioral changes. It can harm the lungs (Tashkin, 1990; Sarafian et al., 1999; Roth et al., 1998); impair short-term memory (Heishman et al., 1997; Fletcher et al., 1996), verbal skills (Block and Ghoneim, 1993), and judgment (Graham et al., 1998); and distort perception (Ameri, 1999; Patrick and Struve, 2000). It may also weaken the immune system and increase the likelihood of developing cancer (Zhu et al., 2000; Zhang et al., 1999). Finally, the use of marijuana by very young teens may have a profoundly negative effect upon their development (Brook et al., 2001; Green and Ritter, 2000; Brook et al., 1999). We need to do a better job educating people on the harmful effects of marijuana use.

Although it may sometimes seem like nothing works to reduce substance abuse by adolescents, the results of research are actually quite promising. In a study that compared treatment approaches, researchers found that multidimensional family therapy (MDFT), which involves individual therapy and family therapy, produced better treatment outcomes than did adolescent group therapy (AGT) or multifamily education intervention (MEI), a treatment delivered in sessions involving more than one family. At the end of treatment, 42 percent of MDFT, 25 percent of AGT, and 22 percent of MEI decreased drug use, and drug use declined further in the twelve months following treatment. Liddle (2001) states, "Those receiving MDFT showed the most improvement in drug use and academic performance, followed by AGT, then MEI." Parental involvement is key to the adolescent's recovery.

Like women's treatment, the process of treating adolescents is essentially the same as it is with adult males. We use the same counseling techniques and strategies. What differs are the complicating factors of youth. We need to take into consideration their stage of development. The mind-set of the adolescent is very different from that of an adult — particularly the impact of peer pressure and the role of the family of origin. In addition, medications must be used with restraint, given that we know little about the long-term impact of medication on children. Younger counselors clearly serve as role models to adolescents and therefore must be even more cognizant of their behavior at all times. Work with adolescents can be physically challenging, especially in a residential setting where the counselor may be expected to play sports with them. When working with youth, the counselor needs to coordinate treatment not only with the team within the setting but also with various external systems — parents, guidance counselors, social service agencies, pediatricians, and so forth. This is very time-consuming and, at times, frustrating. Despite the time and frustration, no other work is more rewarding than that done with children. The need for well-trained counselors to work with adolescents continues to grow. Hopefully many now entering the field will consider working with this population.

RECOVERY COUNSELING OVERVIEW

A Developmental Model as a Framework of Understanding

Most students of addictions counseling want to know what the counselor actually does to help the client give up the addictive substance or behavior. They are asking about the process and the techniques of addictions counseling. In attempting to organize this process of recovery for the students, using Erik Erikson's (1982) stages of psychosocial development as a framework, I have developed a model developmental treatment plan (see pp. 116–118 below).

Most people in the field will accept that recovery, like addiction itself, is a process. Recovery therapy involves facilitating the patient's growth and development through the phases of recovery. A developmental conception of recovery is not new. The best-known model of recovery is that of Gorski and Miller (1982). These authors developed a model describing a process of recovery from alcohol and drug addiction. They present "developmental periods" from pretreatment to maintenance.

So why do we need a new developmental model based on the work of Erik Erikson? The old models do not capture both the developmental process and the tasks of recovery. Hopefully, the new model will communicate the essence of therapy with addicted individuals: both the developmental and psychosocial growth process and the content (concrete tasks and skill development) in such a way that the reader can become an effective addictions counselor by utilizing this information.

Erikson depicts not only the tasks of each stage but also the internal psychological crises and personal strengths of each stage. Each stage presents the client with an opportunity to move forward or the unfortunate possibility of moving backward. For instance, the resolution in early childhood of the autonomy versus shame and doubt crisis, if positively resolved, results in the emergence of the human strength of *will*, but if negatively resolved will result in *compulsion* and *impulsivity*.

The most important concept to understand is that addictions counseling involves more than knowing what tasks the client needs to complete in order to stop engaging in the addictive behavior. Recovery is a lifelong process, and the client needs to acquire not only the tools or skills to stop using the addictive substance or engaging in the addictive behavior but also the personal strengths to remain stopped and to move on to a fulfilling life. At every step in the client's recovery we, as addictions counselors, have the potential to help the client develop another strength. In order to do that we need to view each step in the process both in the short term and long run. Not only must the client not drink "one day at a time" but he also needs to develop qualities of hope, will, and love within the context of a recovery program.

A second concept inherent in Erikson's model is that humans need to resolve one stage positively before they can move on to the next stage. For instance, we need to positively resolve the stage of trust versus mistrust in order to move on to a positive resolution of the next stage of autonomy versus shame and doubt. The easiest way to grasp this concept is by considering the connection between identity and intimacy. Most people would agree that we need a sense of who we are (identity) before we can choose a partner with whom we are compatible (intimacy).

Developmental Process and Tasks of Recovery

Almost every treatment objective or assignment has two purposes: the obvious task of giving up the compulsion and the second goal of developing a strength or resolving a crisis. The following example illustrates this concept. Patients in treatment centers often complain about arbitrary rules. For instance, one patient was insisting that she did not have to go to exercise class on a particular day. There are two therapeutic bases for the rule that a patient needs to go to exercise class. The first is obvious: physical exercise is good for recovery because it burns calories, relieves stress, and gets us in touch with our physical selves.

But an equally important basis is the process of growth in recovery. The more the patient is willing to take on such onerous tasks, the more motivated she is to sobriety. Not only that but it is in the process of seeing herself performing these disliked tasks that the patient begins to realize her willingness to do anything to stay sober. The developing belief is: "Sobriety must be important to me if I am willing to do this in spite of my not wanting to do it."

Moreover, the patient is learning that she is not an exception; she is not unique when it comes to the disease of addiction. She is learning that she suffers from the same disease as everyone else in the treatment facility. Finally, the patient needs to, perhaps for the first time in her life, have faith that someone knows what is best for her until she gets sober.

The Recovery Process in a Nutshell

We will get to the specifics, but let us first review some general guidelines regarding the stages and the process of recovery presented in the model treatment plan. The first five stages are specific to recovery; the last two refer to getting on with life while maintaining sobriety. When the client enters treatment, he may deny that the substance is *the problem*. He continues to blame his job, his wife, his kids. He then learns through education about the disease that alcohol and drugs are *the problem*.

The client may admit at this point that he is more dependent on the drug than he ought to be, but it takes a while before he *admits* that he is an alcoholic and even longer before he *accepts* that he is an alcoholic. Once he can accept that he lost control over his use then he can rid himself of some guilt over his alcohol-related behavior.

In time, the client can identify himself as alcoholic and identify with other recovering people (for example, through a self-help group). This further explains his behavior and facilitates the identity process. He then has other strengths available such as purpose and competence. "My first priority is staying sober, and I can do that if I continue to listen and take suggestions" sums up the belief we, as counselors, are promoting.

These strengths then generalize to other areas: career, friends, and family. The client discovers he can socialize, do his job, and perform sexually while not under the influence of alcohol or drugs. These strengths are available for still further development of identity and intimacy.

Generally, when your client first enters counseling a negative resolution of the crises presented by Erikson is evident. The client is withdrawn, mistrustful, and filled with shame, doubt, guilt, feelings of being "less than" or inferior, identity confusion, and isolation. I will call this negative resolution and presence of negative characteristics *a state* versus a personality *trait* because most of this condition is *temporary* and *a result* (not a cause) of years of addiction.

Prioritizing Treatment Issues

One question I am asked time and time again in the course of teaching addictions counseling has to do with the timing of issues in treatment. Students want to know the order in which they should treat client issues. Most useful in this regard is Maslow's (1970) hierarchical theory of motivation. Maslow proposed that human desires (i.e., motives) are innately given and are arranged in an ascending hierarchy of priority or potency. The needs are, in order of their potency:

1. basic physiological needs;
2. safety needs;
3. belongingness and love needs;
4. self-esteem needs; and
5. self-actualization needs or the need for personal fulfillment.

To Maslow's hierarchy of needs, we can add a simple parallel hierarchy of treatment issues:

1. detoxification;
2. abstinence;
3. belongingness and love, group identification;
4. self-acceptance in sobriety; and
5. personal fulfillment.

Underlying Maslow's scheme is the assumption that low-order needs must be at least somewhat satisfied before an individual can become aware of or motivated by higher-order needs. Gratification of needs lower in the hierarchy allows for awareness of and motivation by needs occurring higher in the hierarchy. What this suggests, for our purposes as counselors, is that we do not work on self-actualization while a person is starving to death and we do not work on self-acceptance or childhood issues while the person is in danger of killing herself with alcohol and drugs. Applying this same theory, if a client focuses on issues that are not relevant to her need level, you can be quite certain that she is in denial and resisting treatment.

Table 7–1
Erikson's Chart of Psychosocial Crises

Developmental stages		*Crises*
Young adulthood	VI	Intimacy versus isolation
		Love versus exclusivity
Adolescence	V	Identity versus identity confusion
		Fidelity versus repudiation
School age	IV	Industry versus inferiority
		Competence versus inertia
Play age	III	Initiative versus guilt
		Purpose versus inhibition
Early childhood	II	Autonomy versus shame, doubt
		Will versus compulsion
Infancy	I	Basic trust versus mistrust
		Hope versus withdrawal

Source: Erik H. Erikson, *The Life Cycle Completed* (New York: W. W. Norton, 1982), 32–33.

Table 7–2
Doyle Pita's Recovery Treatment Plan

STAGE I: INITIATING TREATMENT

Process: Psychosocial crisis: Trust versus mistrust
            Potential strengths: Hope and trust versus withdrawal
            Therapeutic process: Asking for and accepting help

Task: Admitting: "I cannot control use of alcohol/drugs."

Goal: Agreement on treatment goal: stopping compulsion

Strengths needed to move on to next stage: Trust and hope

STAGE II: STOPPING THE COMPULSION

Process: Psychosocial crisis: Autonomy versus shame, doubt
            Potential strengths: Will versus compulsion
            Therapeutic process: "I am willing to try."
                                      "I trust you."
Tasks: Follow treatment plan
            Separating from active loved ones and friends
            Working on Step One: Admitting loss of control
            "I will not use drugs/alcohol."
            "I will attend individual and group therapy and A.A."
            "I will get a sponsor."

Goal: To stay sober one day at a time

Strengths needed to move on to next stage: Trust, hope, and will

STAGE III: WORKING AND PLAYING SOBER

Process: Psychosocial crisis: Initiative versus guilt
                                      Industry versus inferiority
            Potential strengths: Purpose versus inhibition
                                      Competence versus inertia
            Therapeutic process: "I admit that I have the disease."
                                      "My purpose is to stay sober."
                                      "I am a worthwhile person."
Tasks: Psychoeducation
            Working on first three steps
            Returning to work as a recovering person
            Learning to parent sober and noncodependently
            Learning to play, enjoy leisure time, relax, have fun

Goal: Learning to work and play sober

Strengths needed to move on to next stage: Trust, hope, will, purpose,
competence

STAGE IV: IDENTITY DEVELOPMENT SPECIFIC TO SOBRIETY

Process: Psychosocial crisis: Identity versus identity confusion
          Potential strengths: Fidelity versus repudiation
          Therapeutic process: Faith in recovery
                                 Faith in sober self
                                 Faith in higher power
                                 "I am trustworthy."
                                 "I am worthy of respect."

Tasks: Identify and challenge irrational beliefs about self
          Accepting: "I am a recovering alcoholic/addict."
          Learn to accept and care for self
          Work on self-esteem and express feelings about self
          Working Steps Two and Three

Goal: To admit and accept: "I am an alcoholic."
          To begin to identify a spiritual self

Strengths needed to move on to next stage: Trust, hope, will, purpose, competence, faith

STAGE V: INTIMACY DEVELOPMENT SPECIFIC TO SOBRIETY

Process: Psychosocial crisis: Intimacy (in friendships) versus isolation
          Potential strengths: Love (in sobriety) versus exclusivity
          Therapeutic process: Learning about relationships
                                 Honesty and trustworthiness
                                 Expressing feelings to others
                                 Taking risks
                                 Giving and getting needs met

Tasks: Working on relapse prevention
          Getting honest
          Joining a self-help group
          Joining a Step group
          Expressing feelings in a therapy group
          Asking for something
          Learning assertion skills
          Making new sober friends
          Socializing with friends, family, relatives
          Recognizing and giving up codependent behaviors

Goal: To gain socialization and relationship skills

Strengths needed to move on to next stage: Trust, hope, will, purpose, competence, faith, love

STAGE VI: IDENTITY DEVELOPMENT

Process: Psychosocial crisis: Identity versus identity confusion
           Potential strengths: Identity (sense of self) and fidelity
                                          versus repudiation
           Therapeutic process: Learning about self
                                      Self in relation to family of origin
                                      Self in relation to immediate family
                                      Relevance of roles to present identity

Tasks: Giving up other obsessive-compulsive behaviors: food,
              cigarettes, workaholism
           Identifying family-of-origin issues: alcoholism,
              sexual abuse, abandonment
           Identifying feelings about childhood issues
           Giving up old family role: scapegoat, mascot, hero
           Identifying career-related strengths and goals
           Furthering education, making career changes

Goals: To discover who I am now, my strengths and needs

Strengths needed to move on to next stage: Trust, hope, will, purpose,
competence, faith, love, identity

STAGE VII: INTIMACY IN LOVE RELATIONSHIPS

Process: Psychosocial crisis: Intimacy versus isolation
           Potential strengths: Mature love versus role-defined love
           Therapeutic process: Moving from egoistic to mature intimacy

Tasks: Preventing substitute addictions: smoking, eating, sex
           New view of current love relationships
           Giving up unhealthy love relationships
           Choosing healthy new partners
           Getting needs met and giving love
           Accepting partners
           Dealing with codependence with love partners
           Learning to take the perspective of another
           Learning to be less self-centered

Goal: To be able to love in a healthy, mutually satisfying way

= T W E L V E =

STAGE I

Initiating Treatment

Stage I lasts from one day to three months and consists of the actively addicted individual's initiating treatment and agreeing to *try* to stop engaging in the addictive behavior. The primary goal for Stage I, then, is to break through the client's denial regarding his use of alcohol and drugs. The client or patient does not have to believe that he is an alcoholic in order to agree that he needs to do something about the role of the substance in his life. We only need to get the client to see that his drinking is a problem and causes problems for him. We can then pose the following question: "You agree that alcohol causes all these problems and yet you maintain that you do not *need* alcohol. So *if* alcohol is *not* that important to you, then why not give it up?"

We may share with the client our belief that he is an alcoholic, based on the concrete evidence before us and our experience as addictions specialists. However, we are not going to *demand* that the client admit that he is an alcoholic. Believing that one has a problem with alcohol is easier to accept at this point than is believing that one is an alcoholic — with all of the stigma that is attached to that label. If you begin fighting with your client, he probably will not listen to you because you do not yet have a therapeutic relationship. You will sound no different from that nagging spouse, friend, or parent who insists that he sees things her way.

Three Aspects of Self

The client and counselor are always working on all three aspects of self: emotional, spiritual, and cognitive. The relative dominance of one

119

aspect over another varies depending on the point in recovery, the setting at the moment (A.A. or counselor's office), and the approach of the counselor (one will focus on the spiritual aspect early on and another will focus on the cognitive aspect). The goal is simply to get the client to agree to stop using alcohol or drugs, and the effectiveness of the approach at this point in recovery has a lot to do with what the client is willing to "hear."

In my experience, most clients who are just initiating treatment are doing so partly because they choose to and partly because they are pressured into it. These clients simply want the pain to stop, and they want to get people off their backs. They do not necessarily believe that they need to give up alcohol, and they do not necessarily believe in a God or a higher power. They do not even necessarily believe that there is life without alcohol or drugs.

Whether we are talking about inpatient or outpatient treatment, the focus is on the cognitive aspect of self: educating the client about the disease concept, teaching him how to identify his faulty beliefs about the role of alcohol and drugs in his life, helping him explore his beliefs about what got him into treatment (e.g., religious beliefs, personal responsibility, outside stressors), and, most importantly, showing him what he needs to do in order to feel better. We are helping the client to identify the beliefs he has and teaching him how to challenge those beliefs.

Beliefs about alcohol that should be challenged early in treatment include: "Alcohol *is not a* problem." "Alcohol or drugs are the *best* and *only* way to solve emotional problems." "I cannot stand not having a drink." A belief about self to be challenged is: "I am worthless because I am an alcoholic." More of these beliefs, as well as ways to challenge such beliefs, are offered by Ellis et al. (1988).

The primary cognitive component, however, has to do with the belief about trusting and not trusting, and this belief develops within the context of the client-counselor relationship. So the client-counselor relationship is already important. The psychosocial crisis for Stage I is trust versus mistrust. The potential personal strengths to come out of this stage are *hope* and *trust*. The relational aspect involves the client's seeing that he needs help, asking for help, and accepting help. If the client is to accept these new beliefs regarding alcohol and drugs, then he must have some trust in the source: You.

We have previously discussed the personal qualities that contribute to the client's trusting the counselor: empathy, respect, care, and unconditional acceptance. We do not have to love our client or accept his behavior; we simply have to accept him as a human being and care about his getting better. If we batter our client with the label "alcoholic," "drug addict," or "drunk" before he even has a reason to care about what we are saying, then he is going to use his anger at our labels for a reason not to hear anything. If we are judgmental and beat down our client, he will not be able to get up and get sober. Remember, our client has been beaten by the best of them, including himself. We need to sound different from the others.

We need to offer the patient the "hope" that things will get better *if* he stops using addictive substances. We are saying in effect: "You can trust me. There is a way out for you, and I can show it to you. Once I show you how to quit using and stay sober, you are going to have to make the commitment to follow through." Whether he believes you has to do with whether he perceives you as trustworthy and also how entrenched his denial system is. We are never wholly responsible for breaking through the denial system of another. But there is no question that we can facilitate the client's choice to give sobriety a shot. There is also no question that if we perceive our client as hopeless then she will gain no trust or hope from her relationship with us; she will simply feel more hopeless than ever.

The importance of the relational and spiritual aspects become more evident as the client progresses through recovery. The relational and spiritual aspects impact on the very core of the recovering person. She begins to ask questions such as: "Am I an honest person? Am I trustworthy? Am I going to work on gaining the trust of others? Am I worthy of a loving spouse? Am I worthy as a parent?" Because one cannot escape either herself or her higher power, these aspects are crucial in the development of honesty. This personal quality of honesty is put to the test in sobriety again and again.

Stage I Tasks

Let us deal first with the typical case in Stage I. The client enters treatment believing that he needs help. He may not be willing to admit that alcohol is *the* problem, but he is willing to admit that alcohol is *a* problem. In this case, usually the client simply agrees to the treatment plan within the first couple of sessions.

The primary task of Stage I is the development and signing of the treatment plan. An excellent book I now use in my course, and highly recommend, is *The Addictions Treatment Planner* (Perkinson and Jongsma, 2001). A treatment plan is essential to effective treatment; it benefits everyone involved. The patient has a road map. The provider benefits because the counselor is forced to think through the objectives and goals. There is clear documentation of treatment, protecting the provider from lawsuits from patients. The treatment team benefits because the treatment plan is a way of communicating between members of the team. Finally, the substance abuse treatment profession benefits because its counselors are providing measurable evidence of treatment success. The treatment plan reinforces the commitment of the client to work with the counselor in achieving goals. The concrete proof of a contract between client and counselor is the treatment plan. In signing the treatment plan, the client is saying in effect, "I admit that I have a problem and I need help. I am taking responsibility for getting the help I need." In the signing of the treatment plan by you and the client, the two of you are recognizing the beginnings of and commitment to a mutually agreed-upon plan of action.

The components of the treatment plan vary depending upon the individual case and the point at which the person is in recovery, but the common element is the client's statement that "I will try not to use alcohol and drugs." A sample treatment plan for Stage I for both inpatient and outpatient treatment can be found in appendix B (p. 169). In this sample plan, we can see that the client is agreeing to attend individual and group therapy and is agreeing to attend A.A. or another appropriate self-help group. She does not have to believe that she is an alcoholic to go to meetings. She may also be agreeing to make some changes with regard to work or family. In the typical case, the individual will agree to stop engaging in the addictive behavior but will continue to disagree with the specific methods of accomplishing this. For instance, she may disagree with the number of A.A. meetings or the goal of not becoming intimately involved with a new partner for the first year of sobriety.

The client progresses to Stage II when she admits to a loss of control over the substance and agrees to try not to use alcohol and drugs. In order to do so, the client has achieved some level of trust and hope regarding living without the use of drugs and alcohol. The length of Stage I depends on factors such as denial; length of drugging or drinking history; external motivators such as spouse, job, and children; and number of losses. This phase covers the period between the point at which the client initiates therapy and agrees to the treatment plan or, alternatively, drops out of treatment on her own or is referred elsewhere.

Clients may agree to try to stop using alcohol or drugs but may be doing so out of compliance, not because they have positively resolved the Stage I crisis. Compliance sometimes results from the counselor's verbally beating up on the patient. The client will agree to try to stop drinking simply to get the counselor off his back. Compliance is a problem that does not become apparent until Stage II and is discussed in that section.

Resistance and Solutions in Stage I

It should come as no surprise that not all clients agree to try to stop drinking or drugging. What can we do if the client *refuses* to *try* to stop using addictive substances? The client is in denial and maintains denial despite our efforts. If the client refuses to try to stop and we are convinced that he must stop, we can employ several techniques in Stage I to attempt to break through the client's denial.

We may try an intervention, essentially repeating a step taken to get the client into treatment in the first place. We may bring in family, friends, physician, and employers to break through the client's denial that alcohol or drugs are a problem. Sometimes, once the client has entered treatment, we can gain the cooperation of loved ones who are now willing to come in and confront the client.

Use of Contracts

If you do not have any leverage, such as the threat of a job or family loss, you may try an "If-Then" contract. In this contract, the client attempts to prove to you that he is not an alcoholic by controlling his alcohol intake. The two of you set a limit as to what constitutes "social drinking." The contract between you and the client states: *"If I* go beyond my limit of (for example) two glasses of wine two times per week, *then I will* agree I do not have control over my drinking and I will try to stop drinking." If your assessment is correct and the client is an alcoholic, then he will not be able to maintain this limit because, by definition, he has lost control over alcohol or drugs.

There are several sets of circumstances in which the "If-Then" contract would not be recommended. One involves a third party that has abstinence as a condition of its contract with you and the client, for instance, where there is a return-to-work agreement or a licensing board involved. A second case is one in which the client is bargaining with the use of illicit drugs. We cannot agree to the use of illegal drugs for ethical reasons. Another case is the physically sick patient or the suicidal patient. The suicidal patient is especially risky, particularly when he is on medication. If a client is on medication and consuming alcohol, we might involve the prescribing physician in helping break through the denial.

The client may be in too much denial to make any kind of commitment to sobriety. At this point, the best thing we can do for the client is to admit that we cannot help him and to suggest that he needs some other form of treatment or that no treatment will help until he is willing to do something to help himself. We must not let our egos get in the way of our admitting our own powerlessness over the active addict who refuses to ask for our help.

THIRTEEN

STAGE II

Stopping the Compulsion

Stage II consists of the recovering individual's stopping the addictive behavior and staying stopped for at least a six-month period. The primary treatment goal is to provide the external and internal structure necessary to help the client not use the addictive substance or engage in the addictive behavior (such as gambling or sex addiction). At this very early stage of recovery, we help hold the client's environment stable so that the healing process may begin. The A.A. slogan "Keep it simple" is the one we need to heed. Establishing this external structure may take from three to six months.

The psychosocial crisis of Stage II is autonomy versus shame and doubt. The potential strength is will versus compulsion. The three aspects of self begin to emerge. In the context of the counseling relationship, the client is helped to look at her cognitive, spiritual, and emotional/relational self. In so doing, she begins to resolve the question of whether she is an alcoholic. The client is asked: "What are you willing to do to get sober?" As the feelings of shame and doubt emerge, we help the client see that she can get sober, and sobriety is the only way to rid herself of shame and doubt.

In the counseling relationship, we help the client to see that there is only one alternative to living in this fear of learning how to live a sober life. There is great indecision at this point between choosing to try to get sober and choosing to simply reactivate the compulsion. The client is asking himself: "Can I be autonomous and move forward to a positive life where I take responsibility for getting my needs met in a healthy way?" Or, alternatively, "Will I remain dependent upon my addiction as a way of avoiding life? What if I fail? If I try and fail, then I will be a failure, a loser." This decision making process is one that we all go through: Shall I risk letting go of what I have and move on, or should I hang on to what I've got even though it doesn't make me happy? We see this indecisiveness in decisions regarding work and relationships. Is there something better out there for me? I referred to this process of letting go and hanging on as the "Dumbo Dilemma" (Doyle Pita, 1993). The compulsion that addicts hang on to is like the feather that the Disney character Dumbo held on to, believing that it was keeping him afloat. This process is also captured in the expression that you can't make it to second base with one foot still on first.

We need to take a leap of faith to gain the courage to let go of the past and move on to new beginnings. Relapse frequently occurs when clients are in transition from one phase to the next — when they move from a halfway house to an apartment, when they are just about to finish up their probation, when they get their kids back, when they get that job promotion, when they reunite with their significant other. They are so afraid of failure that they would rather slide back into what is miserable but familiar. As counselors, our task is to reinforce self-efficacy, to build the client's belief that she can make it in life without her addiction.

Three Aspects of Self

The client's beliefs about his ability to control his use of alcohol or drugs are challenged through cognitive techniques within the counseling relationship. The goal is for the client to admit his powerlessness over alcohol. This admission opens up feelings of shame and doubt as the person sees he is vulnerable. He sees that it is the drug and not himself that has been in control of his life. But he must be willing to work at this self-awareness. The client learns the difference between willingness and willfulness. Willfulness is "doing it his way," "being in control." Willingness involves giving up enough control so that he is open to the suggestions and feedback of others. He is scared because he recognizes on an emotional level that if he has lost control over alcohol in the past, then he can lose control over alcohol again.

We continue to work with the client on the concept of disease and loss of control, and how these relate to the client personally. This kind of personalized education is called psychoeducation. You begin to challenge the "badness" of being alcoholic. You challenge misperceptions by asking questions such as: "What does it mean to be an alcoholic?" "What does an alcoholic look like?" "How do you know that you are an alcoholic?" The client needs to be convinced that having one drink is not worth the risk of losing something important. You continue to work on Step One, showing the client how his life has become unmanageable as a result of alcohol or drug use.

The spiritual aspect becomes increasingly dominant as the client considers Step Two: "Came to believe that a Power greater than ourselves could restore us to sanity." The client is attending a Twelve Step program and is faced with the question of a higher power every time he goes to a meeting, if he is listening. The client is beginning to see that he is powerless over alcohol, and in admitting his powerlessness he will begin to seek something else to believe in. Can he trust that his God will restore his sanity *if* he admits his powerlessness? Almost everyone has feelings and thoughts about God or a higher power. One point we need to examine with our client is the difference between religion and spirituality. The client's last contact with God may have been as an angry teenager forced to attend church. Many people feel angry and let down by their God. We need to explore this difference with the client and inquire about the image the client has of God.

Clients often feel relief in recognizing they have a disease because they are no longer to blame for their alcohol-related behavior. They are not bad; they merely have a bad disease. But then they blame God for giving them the disease in the first place. The client needs to explore the helpfulness of this belief for his recovery. Forgiveness, not anger, is going to give him freedom from his addiction. The client's higher power needs to become a source of positive strength and safety, not a source of punishment and shame. Forgiveness takes time; a client cannot all of a sudden forgive God, himself, or other people in his life.

If you are not comfortable with the spiritual aspect, you may consider referring your client to clergy in his community as an adjunct to your counseling. Although we can provide internal and external structure through meetings and new belief systems, the safety provided by a belief in a God relates to the spiritual self of the person and gives the person a feeling of safety, security, and acceptance. The client believes on an emotional level that God will help her, if she asks.

Emotional/rational aspects, other than what we have already discussed, are not the focus. The client needs to hear that he is doing all he can do to get sober. The client needs to hear positive acceptance. The client will describe her feelings as "being on a roller coaster." We do not do a lot of feeling work at this point because the clients do not have the coping mechanisms needed to deal with feelings. If they are encouraged to get in touch with their anger or pain, having no way to handle the feelings, the clients will respond as they always have, by drowning the feelings with alcohol. They simply need to move forward within the structure that we have provided and with the feelings of trust, hope, and autonomy that we are positively reinforcing. We do not deny the client's feelings; we recognize the feelings, but how we deal with them depends upon the urgency of the feelings and where the person is in recovery.

If the client expresses feelings about us or feelings about people in his life *today*, then we help the client to develop more realistic expectations so that he does not run (escape in a self-destructive way) with his feelings. We can do this effectively by using RET. The client needs some quick and easy ways to deal with the feelings that come up in daily living, feelings that, in the past, led him straight to the nearest liquor store. For example, a client often gets angry because people in his life do not seem to appreciate how difficult it is for him to stay sober. Co-workers may order alcoholic drinks when they are out for dinner, or a spouse may leave some wine in the refrigerator or invite friends over who bring alcohol with them. We need to teach the client to identify and challenge his irrational expectations about other's behavior. We are asking in effect: "Why *should* the people in your life act the way you want them to act? It would be nice if they did but, of course, they will not always or even usually act the way you want them to. How can you not upset yourself about that reality?"

Expression of feelings within the context of the therapeutic relationship is encouraged because they can be handled safely within that relationship. This is one way the client is going to learn how to have intimate relationships. For example, clients often feel hurt and angry when they discover that we are not going to satisfy their dependency needs. We need to explore these feelings and expectations with the client.

In contrast to these feelings in the "here and now," feelings about past events, especially childhood events such as sexual abuse, cannot effectively be dealt with until the client has some means of handling these feelings. Moreover, we must always remember that our treatment objectives are dependent upon the stage of recovery. In Stage II, the goal is simply to stay sober, and in counseling the addict we do whatever facilitates that goal. We acknowledge how painful such childhood events must be, but we point out that now is not the best time to begin working through that pain. We can say to our client: "The more sober time you have, the deeper the issues you will be able to handle."

Stage II Tasks

The primary tasks of Stage II involve the client's adherence to the treatment plan. Is the client following the spirit as well as the letter of the treatment plan? Is the client taking steps to separate from active friends or does he "just happen" to run into his old buddies? Is he making a conscious effort not to start romantic or sexual involvements or is he already attending sober dances and spending his time at meetings checking out potential female partners? Does the client stay away from specified hangouts but then stop in at a new club or pool hall?

We need to constantly monitor the client's progress toward the treatment goals. We need to check in on the client's experience of his other treatment modalities. We can do this by exploring the client's beliefs and behaviors. The client is responding to his feelings about A.A. and alcoholics. Can he identify with their stories? If not, why not? Is he choosing meetings at which the alcoholics are so unlike himself that he does not have to identify with their stories? If he is addicted to other drugs, is he attending Narcotics Anonymous meetings? Is it okay to be an alcoholic but not to be a drug addict? How does he feel about his sitting among the alcoholics? Does he sit at the back of the room or up front? Has he raised his hand to speak? Has he introduced himself to others? Does he have a sponsor? Has he asked for help? Is he attending consistently or is he beginning to slack off?

What are his feelings about group counseling, the group leader, and other members? Whom does he trust, whom does he mistrust, and on what does he base this judgment? What is his behavior in group therapy? Is he an active member or a passive observer? Has he shared his feelings about being in treatment? Has he taken any risks? Has he cried? Has he confronted another member? Or, alternatively, is he just along for the ride, with participation limited to throwing out a few A.A. slogans? These are questions we need to explore with our clients again and again because the answers tell us whether the client is simply complying or whether he is beginning to process what is going on.

We can help provide the external structure necessary to allow the client to begin to heal. As the client recognizes her loss of control and the unmanageability of her life, she is scared. We respond by suggesting ways she can structure her life in the form of attending A.A. meetings, developing an A.A. network, getting a sponsor, enjoying leisure-time activities, and obtaining individual and group counseling. We help develop internal structure by facilitating the development of healthy beliefs and challenging irrational beliefs. Slogans such as "Take it easy" and "One day at a time" are safe and reassuring to someone whose life has fallen apart.

Resistance and Solutions in Stage II

Resistance at Stage II generally results from the failure of the client to admit that he does have a problem with alcohol and must stop engaging in the compulsion if he is to get better. The denial system is still intact. The client agreed to try to quit, but chances are he was complying rather than believing that he needed to give up the addictive substance. The behavioral signs that denial is still intact become obvious over time, eventually erupting in the client's use of alcohol or another drug.

How do we know when the client is retreating to his denial system? One of the first signs is the client's failure to follow through with the treatment plan objectives. This is one reason we need a very concrete treatment plan. The client may have agreed to attend five meetings a week and now is only attending one or two. We need to address this "slippage" immediately.

We need to return again and again to the client's beliefs about his alcohol or drug use and the insidious belief that he can drink again. We need to go back and ask the same questions: "How do you know you are an alcoholic? What would you do if you did have a drink? What do you think would happen? Who would you tell if you had a drink? What would you do about it?" Because the addicted individual has lived in the extremes for so long, he applies this thinking to his own setbacks in recovery. If he has a drink he believes: "It is all over. I blew it, I might as well get really drunk now. There is no sense in going back to counseling now that I have blown it." Uncovering and teaching the client how to challenge this nonsense is essential to recovery.

The client needs to believe that no matter what he does, he needs to get back on track. If he drinks, he must tell someone immediately: his counselor, his sponsor, his group. Keeping such a secret is deadly to recovery. If the client says that he would not tell anyone because of his shame, then we can show the client that he has not accepted his loss of control over the drug; he has not accepted his alcoholism. They say that alcoholism is a disease of relapse, and we need to show our client that he is not bad because he is an alcoholic. The question is: "What are you going to do about it now that it has happened?" The only thing the client can do now is put down the alcohol or drug and try again.

Use of Contracts

One way to deal with the fear of, or actuality of, slips and relapses is with a contract or written agreement, that is, a written emergency plan stating specifically what the client will do if she drinks or takes drugs. This is especially important for clients who have attempted suicide or who say they will kill themselves if they drink again. Some clients will tell you, "I don't have another recovery in me." They believe that this belief, magically, is keeping them sober. It is not keeping them sober, and relapses are always a possibility; they need to prepare for that possibility before it happens. We must discuss slips and relapse with all our clients, regardless of whether they are following through with the treatment plan. When a slip does occur, the client has a plan to follow that will lead him back to counseling and sobriety.

Slips and relapses need to be treated as learning experiences. The client needs to be asked what he has learned from the slip, what he thinks needs to change in the treatment plan and within himself. If the client continues to fail to follow through, then we know that denial is still intact.

I am frequently asked: How many times does the client need to slip or relapse before you decide that treatment is not working for this client at this time? That is, of course, a very individual decision and has to do with the specifics of the case. Is the client under a "Return-to-Work" agreement that states how slips and relapses are to be handled? Is the client in a high-risk occupation in which there is a likelihood that someone is going to get hurt if our client uses drugs or alcohol on the job? Obviously, if our client is an airline pilot, bus driver, or medical professional, then the risk is greater. We have less leeway in deciding how to handle slips and relapses when we are dealing with clients in high-risk occupations.

We need to consider whether the problem is in the treatment plan or in the client's behavior. Since we are only talking about the first three to six months (getting the structure in place and seeing if it works), it should become pretty obvious in a short period of time whether the client is going to respond to this treatment method.

If the client slips more than once in the first three months, the prognosis for sobriety does not look good. How you respond to the slip depends on whether the client was following the treatment plan and had a slip anyway or was not following the treatment plan. If the client stopped in at the local pub to order a Coke and a sandwich, then the problem is pretty obvious. He is not following the spirit of the treatment plan; denial is intact. We need to discuss with the client the question of why he is setting himself up to drink. If the client was following the treatment plan and still had a slip, then that is a different problem requiring further changes in the treatment plan.

FOURTEEN

STAGE III

Working and Playing Sober

Stage III involves the client's fitting work and play into sobriety. This stage begins anywhere from one to three months after beginning treatment and continues to one year. The time depends, in part, on the type of occupation the client has and whether the client is able to return to that job at this time. Learning to play sober needs to begin within the first three months. The process of this stage is the psychosocial crisis of initiative versus guilt. The potential strengths are purpose and competence versus inhibition and inertia. The client is saying, "I have stopped drinking. Now what? I know how to be an alcoholic in recovery. Now how do I deal with the real world?" The client needs to begin to rid herself of guilt because guilt and feelings of being "less than" tie up the recovering person's energy and keep her from moving forward. The client is learning to get to know who she is without alcohol or drugs.

Three Aspects of Self

The cognitive aspect continues to be primary. In helping the client rid himself of the guilt, we can focus on the concept of alcoholism. The client did not choose to be an alcoholic and were he not an alcoholic, he would not have done a lot of the hurtful things he has done to others and to himself. The client begins to admit he is alcoholic. Will the client move forward and do what he needs to do to live a sober way of life? Or, alternatively, will he stagnate and regress to the denial that tells him: "It wasn't that bad." "You are not like 'them' (i.e., alcoholics)." "You can learn to control your drinking."

The spiritual aspect comes to the fore as the client reexperiences his fear of others and feelings of shame in returning to social circles and the workplace. You will find that your clients are asking their higher power for help more and more frequently, and most are discovering that they get the help they need when they do ask. They need this feeling of trust in taking on the new challenges of social activities and work. Through this experience they often come to believe in a higher power restoring them to sanity. At this point in recovery, clients will begin returning to church and contacting clergy from their past.

The emotional/relational aspect does not change much during this phase. As a counselor we continue to use cognitive techniques, help the client follow through with the treatment plan, and offer the client our encouragement. We always focus on the client's strengths and potential, and we do a lot of what is called *strength confrontation*, which involves confronting the client with strengths that he denies he has.

Stage III Tasks

Stage III is very task-oriented because this stage involves the client doing a lot of legwork as he expands his recovery sphere to include work and social life. Psychoeducation continues regarding the disease concept, and the client begins to believe, not just intellectually, but emotionally, that he does have the disease of addiction. The process of moving the belief from an intellectual to an emotional level involves working on the first three steps. In addition to this psychological and spiritual work, the client is returning to his workplace as a sober person. He is also returning to his family as a sober parent and to his social life as a sober friend. Learning to work and play sober are major hurdles for the newly recovering person.

Learning to Play in Sobriety

Teaching the client how to play as a sober person is one of the more enjoyable aspects of recovery counseling. There are two types of play in recovery. There is play that involves activities that the client needs to do for fun and relaxation, and there is the play involved in developing a sense of humor about oneself, others, and life in general. I do not think that there is a more essential component in counseling than humor.

Helping the client to lighten up and laugh at his and others' human capacity for making mistakes enables the client to let go of some of his perfectionism and self-criticism. Spontaneity returns, and the client can begin to take risks with himself in the play arena that he is not ready to take in the work arena.

Ellis (1977a, 1977b) has pioneered the use of humor as a method of psychotherapy. Ellis et al. (1988) write, "Humor is often a fine antidote against disturbance and compulsion because it has a powerful emotive as well as cognitive element. Laughter can dramatically jolt your clients out of their self-defeating habits and cleverly push them into anti-addictive action." Perhaps what I find most amazing in my work as a therapist is how a simple phrase or comment given at just the right moment, an unexpected moment, can break through denial in a way that months of empathic listening cannot. The phrase is most useful when it does not fit neatly into the client's belief system.

Humor can challenge our defense system in a way that simple confrontation cannot. Because it is humor, it is not as threatening. Humor allows the person to see things in a totally new light. Think about your own experiences with humor and how it has helped you accept reality. The people I learn the most from and enjoy the most are the ones who push me to see things in a different light; they do this with humor. But remember, as with comedy in general, timing is everything. We need to learn when and what type of humor to use. There is a fine line between "making fun of" the client's beliefs in a way that is shaming and bringing the client along with us to find the humor in his beliefs. Sarcasm is not an appropriate form of humor in the therapeutic setting.

A sense of humor is as important for us, as counselors, as it is for the client. The counselor needs a sense of humor as a survival method in recovery counseling, and she needs a sense of humor to help facilitate the client's use of humor. I do not know whether you can develop a sense of humor on our own. In my experience, those counselors and therapists who are able to survive and thrive in the field of addictions seem to have a well-developed sense of humor. They may have entered the field with it, and it may have also become more developed along the way as an adaptive mechanism. For those who do not have a sense of humor, listening to some of Ellis's (1977b) rational humorous songs, which he uses as a part of psychotherapy with his clients, may be of help in developing one.

Much of human behavior when viewed from the outside is humorous. We can all recall arguing with a loved one over something ridiculous. At the time we are angry, but a month later we cannot even recall what the argument was about. This behavior, in retrospect, looks childish to us, and it is. The person has no perspective at the time; all he can focus on are *his* feelings, *his* wants.

The positive side to childish behavior is that it shows the person can get in touch with what John Bradshaw refers to as the "inner child." Perhaps only an angry, hurt inner child is apparent at first, but in time other aspects will also emerge: the more spontaneous, fun-loving, joyful child. Getting in touch with the inner child serves several functions. The client learns to differentiate between childish and childlike behavior and, knowing the difference, can allow herself to be childlike when appropriate. This introduction to the playful child will help in later stages as the client works on healing the pain of the inner child. By recognizing childish behavior as that of his "inner child" and not that of his "adult" self, the client can begin to learn how to satisfy the needs of the inner child while responding to the situation with his adult self.

The cognitive aspect has to do with the recovering individuals' lack of self-acceptance. Because they do not view themselves as worthy, they are not motivated to do anything for themselves that involves just having fun. The unhealthy belief is this: "I am not worth it. I have already wasted enough time on myself indulging in my addiction. Now it's time for me to work." We need to challenge this belief by showing the client that she is worth it, and that in order for her recovery to continue she needs to learn how to relax and enjoy herself. Also, if the client does not learn how to relax and have fun, she may channel her energy into work or another compulsion, and then we simply have a new addiction.

Clients typically do not have a well-developed concept of fun or leisure that is not connected to drinking or drugging. In treatment planning, we develop play objectives just as we do any other objectives. The activity must not involve alcohol, it is best done with at least one other person, and it needs to be potentially enjoyable for the client. Play can be as simple as going to the movies, going shopping or to a museum, or going out for lunch with a friend.

Play can combine different aspects of the self: social, emotional, and physical, for example, joining a health club. Often we need to encourage our clients to use the health club after they have joined because otherwise they may not take the time. Lost hobbies or sports are also excellent, such as golf, tennis, boating, and roller skating. Drawing out the client's imagination and creativity can be done through photography, art, or dance classes. In time, we need to work on the client to take a vacation, and then we need to plan for her to have fun on her vacation.

Learning to Work Sober

The work area is also very important for the client's self-esteem and self-confidence. The individual needs to develop or reidentify a sense of competence and purpose. As discussed earlier, we need to be aware of many factors in helping the client deal with the career issue. We need to know how the workplace perceives his addiction, or if it even knows about it. We need to know how the client feels about his job, the stresses on the job, and whether he feels safe returning to the same job site and occupation. When, where, and how the person returns to work also has to do with what type of treatment she received and what the insurance company is willing to provide for aftercare (e.g., outpatient group and individual counseling).

The work-specific cognitive aspect in Stage III has to do with challenging feelings of shame and anger, low self-worth, fear of failure, and fear of drinking or drugging on the job. Feelings of shame and guilt connect back to a failure to accept that one is an alcoholic, and that an alcoholic is not a bad person but a person with a disease.

Fear of relapse also has to do with acceptance that one has a disease and needs to plan accordingly to deal with feelings and urges while on the job. Fear of failure on the job has to do with this irrational notion that many people suffer from: "I must do my job perfectly; if I do not, I am a bad, worthless human being."

Another very common issue that crops up along with feelings of worthlessness on the job is assertiveness. Often clients view themselves as second-class citizens and thus do not strike a good balance between putting others' needs above their own and aggressively taking what they need. I recommend working on assertiveness with the client to teach her how to get along with others and still get her professional needs met.

Resistance and Solutions in Stage III

Resistance in Stage III comes in the form of a fearful "I can't" rather than the defiant "I won't" of previous stages. The client is afraid of failing in his tasks of returning to work or play. Because of the level of awareness he has already gained and his relationship with us, the client is less able to use defiance but more able to rely on his old behavior of helpless, hopeless dependence in hopes that we will rescue him. I have discussed possible solutions to this form of resistance under cognitive techniques, but, most simply put, I always come back to the same question: "What are you willing to do to stay sober?" Because it is not that you cannot, it is that you *will not*. Maybe you cannot envision yourself sober for the rest of your life but: "You can ask a friend out for coffee," "You can speak to your boss about getting out of work early on Wednesdays," and so on.

Return-to-Work Issues

Most often the employer does not even know that the employee has received treatment for an addiction. In that case, we work out the recovery plan with the client. When people in the workplace know that the employee is in recovery, this creates a whole new set of issues. In addition to excuses that recovery is interfering with work are the excuses that work is interfering with recovery. Some clients will use recovery as an excuse for not doing their share of the work. Unfortunately, some bosses and employee assistance programs will enable this type of behavior by allowing it to continue. The boss wants to be a "nice guy," and he thinks he is doing all he can to help his employee get back on his feet. The boss does not realize that he is doing a disservice to himself, his company, his other employees, and the recovering person.

The recovering person needs to be held accountable for her share of the work. In addition, she needs to feel as though people have confidence in her abilities and expect her to perform up to her capabilities. Many brilliant and gifted people have talents that are never realized because they have been so "protected" at their workplace. The workplace employees and colleagues are so afraid of losing the person to alcohol or drugs again that they remove all the challenge from that person's career. One of the greatest harms we can do to people is to expect little from them.

The other side of the expectation coin is expecting too much. Another danger in the recovering person's return to work is a "setup" in the workplace. Co-workers may set the person up to fail because they are angry at her or because they want to get her out of their organization. The setting up of a person usually involves overloading her with work or treating her in a negative way because she is an addict. Both can drive the person back to the drug and out of work. For instance, a nurse may be set up by returning her to a hospital floor on which she has access to medication or to a floor where everyone knows she was caught diverting (i.e., stealing) drugs from work and then treat her badly because of that.

We need to find a balance between these two extremes of underworking and overworking the newly recovering employee. The returning person needs to return slowly. She needs to be updated on the events and information she missed while she was away. She needs to be told specifically what her job description is. Medical people need to have either no access or only limited access to psychoactive medication when returning to work, and this needs to be worked out with the direct supervisor. Over time, job restrictions need to be lifted as the returning person gains back her responsibilities. She needs to be shown that she is gaining back the trust of her boss and co-workers. Eventually, the person needs to be considered for and offered promotions based on job performance, just like any other employee.

In addition to work performance expectations are the expectations that the counselor, the workplace, and the client have with regard to recovery. Recovery can take many forms. Employees do not need to get out of work early every night to attend A.A. or group counseling. However, some consideration needs to be given to the employee and her treatment. A request to get out of work early one night a week for treatment purposes is not unreasonable, as long as the employee offers to make up the time. Compromises must be reached to prevent resentment from growing, and it is best if they are reached prior to the person's return to the workplace. Not only can the employer come to resent the recovering person, but co-workers may resent the special treatment she gets and will make the job environment a living hell. Soon the workplace can be operating like one big dysfunctional family. The recovering person will be the scapegoat, a role that is all too familiar and one that can lead back to active addiction.

Use of Contracts

An effective way to deal with return-to-work issues involves drawing up a contract or agreement between the workplace (boss or direct supervisor), the client, and the counselor. An example of a return-to-work agreement is included as appendix C (p. 173). In preparing this contract, each person writes out her specific role and expectations. Compromises are then reached. Each person understands the procedure to be followed when conditions of the contract are broken. Your client knows ahead of time what will happen if she takes a drink or drug. The workplace knows how to deal with work performance problems and whom to contact when there is a problem with which they cannot deal. All those involved feel more comfortable knowing where they stand.

FIFTEEN

STAGES IV AND V

Identity and Intimacy in Recovery

The identity and intimacy development of which we are speaking in Stages IV and V is specific to recovery rather than that which occurs as a function of normal development. For instance, identity in this stage has to do with the recovering person's identity as an alcoholic, not a more general identity question of "Who am I?"

Stage IV: Identity Development Specific to Recovery

The psychosocial crisis of Stage IV is identity versus identity confusion. The potential strength is fidelity versus repudiation. The resolution of the crisis typically occurs during the end of year one and the beginning of year two. The crucial aspect of Stage IV involves the client's *acceptance* that she is an alcoholic. The client is saying, "I am an alcoholic, but I have the tools to know how to deal with my alcoholism and that is okay." This is not to say that the client feels good about being an alcoholic; typically this comes much later in recovery. In fact, there is often a letdown around the first year sober date because the client thinks, "This is the way it is. This is the way my life needs to be in order for me to stay sober." That is pretty overwhelming for the client who has just struggled through the first year.

Nor am I suggesting that the recovering person does not backslide after she has reached this point. Recovery is a process; clients continue to move forward and backward as they are affected by internal and external stressors. Hopefully, they will have learned to cope with stressors without resorting to their addiction. Possibly the biggest mistake we make as therapists is to assume that there is a "cure" for this disease. We begin to move on to other areas, and we neglect the client's sobriety. We need to continue to check in on our client's sobriety even after three years or fifteen years.

On the positive side, the strength that emerges in Stage IV is fidelity. The recovering person has faith in the promises of recovery, faith in a higher power, and faith in the self-help program. A marker of this transition is the client's ability to utilize not only our guidance but also to branch out and use mentors and leaders. The negative potential outcome of this stage is role repudiation: a diffidence or defiance in relation to available identity potential, according to Erikson (1982). The client who does not utilize mentors in the program as part of his *recovery identity* often shows a great deal of anger and begins to put down the membership or attack aspects of the program.

Three Aspects of Self

The spiritual self is primary during Stage IV as the recovering person chooses between turning over her will to a higher power and taking that will back. She struggles with her faith in God, A.A., and herself, as she asks: "Will I accept this identity as an alcoholic or will I return to my denial and believe that I can continue to drink and drug?" This question is, of course, not entirely a conscious one. A marker for this transition is the client's asking for help and letting God decide what the form of help will be rather than asking for specific things. Those who ask for things and express anger when they do not get what they want have not turned over their will.

The cognitive aspect does not change in this stage. You continue to work with the alcoholic in challenging her unhealthy beliefs about self and others. The emotional/relational aspect also continues as in the previous stage. Every client is an individual and responds differently to the first year of sobriety, but there are some general markers. In my experience, clients respond either with joy or sadness to this stage. Those who respond with joy are generally clients who did not make it to a year in their previous sobriety attempts. Those with sadness or apathy tend to be younger, and to them the thought of facing a lifetime of sobriety as they experienced it in the first year is, indeed, sad. The quality of sobriety is obviously higher for those who are enjoying their sobriety, but that does not mean that those clients who are feeling down are in trouble with regard to their recovery. This feeling is less a predictor of future sobriety than an indication of past attempts.

On a cognitive level, we can respond to the overwhelmingness of a lifetime of recovery by pointing out that every year recovery gets better with more rewards. We can also remind the client of the meaning of the A.A. slogan: "One day at a time." Counseling groups and support groups are crucial at this time; in them the recovering person hears that others share these feelings, and the others can reassure the recovering person that as long as she does not drink or drug things will get better.

Stage IV Tasks

In Stage IV the client continues to work with the counselor on challenging unhealthy beliefs about self. The client is learning not only to admit that she is an alcoholic but to accept this fact and learn how to integrate that component of self into her larger identity. With that acceptance, the client begins to focus on taking care of herself. She works on developing self-esteem and expressing her knowledge about self (feelings, wants, and needs). She continues to work on Steps Two and Three as she begins to identify and connect with her spiritual self. Much of the work in Stage IV involves tasks to be completed by the counselor as she deals with various forms of client resistance.

Resistance and Solutions in Stage IV

The client's defiance can present itself in various forms. As in all previous stages, we need to pay attention primarily to the client's behavior and not her words. Behavioral markers include the following: Is the client sticking to the treatment plan? Is the client still afraid of alcohol, as he should be, or has he begun testing his disease by stopping off at the local pub for a Coke or going out with friends to a club after work? Has the client begun to internalize the identity of the A.A. group? Does the client express the "need" for a meeting without your suggesting it? Does the client belong to a group? Do the people in his group have his phone number and do they ask him where he has been when he fails to show up for a meeting? Does he celebrate his one-year sobriety anniversary with his group, or does he fail to do anything on his anniversary?

Erikson speaks of the importance of mentorship in identity development, and we can apply this to recovery as well. The role of mentors is particularly telling because much of the addict's battle has to do with control and defiance against authorities. If this struggle has not been resolved, the client will be unable or unwilling to use mentors. You need to know the answers to the following questions: Does the client have a sponsor, and how does she feel about her sponsor? Does she call her sponsor only when she has things under control? What does your client do when she becomes really stressed and feels like picking up a drink or drug? Does she call you or her sponsor, or does she isolate herself and then tell you about it a week later when she has "fixed it"? How does she feel about other people in the program giving her suggestions or confronting her? Does she utilize feedback by putting it into action, or does she just give it lip service?

As counselors, we are also authority figures, and our clients sometimes react defiantly to our suggestions. If your client does not express anger overtly, she may do it passively. Passive aggression or anger may come in the form of her not following the treatment plan, in her not paying you on time, or in canceling appointments at the last minute. Defiance is often expressed in sarcastic humor. There is nothing wrong with our clients' feeling anger toward us. In fact, if they never feel anger toward us, we may not be hitting the right buttons. Our clients are going to hear feedback that they do not want to consider, and sometimes they are going to get angry at us for pointing out this vulnerability to them. The problem is not the client's anger; it is how the client manages her anger. We need to teach the client how to identify her angry feelings, determine their source, and learn how to express them appropriately (i.e., so that they will be heard).

Is the client doing her homework, or is she making excuses? Does she agree to do her homework and then come back week after week not "having had the time" to follow through? To deal with this resistance we rely on our relationship with the client, which is why it is so important to have established a relationship with the client. Rather than focus on the content (no time to do homework) and spending the session problem solving with the client (scheduling her day for her), we focus on what is going on in the therapeutic relationship. How do these resistant behaviors affect the therapeutic relationship? If the client agrees to homework and then does not do it, we may ask her what this says about her trust in us as a counselor and the strength of her commitment to sobriety.

Slips and Relapses

Slips and relapses need to be used as learning experiences. If the client has stayed sober for a year, we can say that he "has the tools" to not use alcohol or drugs. So why did he use them? We need to focus on what his return to his addictive behavior has to say about his motivation to sobriety and about his level of trust in those who are helping him with his sobriety. For instance, consider the following scenario. A client discusses with you a getaway weekend in which there is the possibility of drug use. The two of you agree that going on the trip would be too risky. In his next session, he reports that he did go on the trip and he did use drugs.

What does such resistance say about your counseling relationship and the client's level of commitment to sobriety? By focusing on the relationship, we avoid blaming the client. The client is responsible for his bad choices, but he is not a bad person. If we focus on "the badness" of our client, our client is going to feel "bad," not badly but *bad.* We cannot beat our client into sobriety; he must go willingly. If your client feels "bad," he will get as angry at you as he did at his parents, and he will then have a reason (albeit irrational) not to trust you.

Splitting

Another sign of resistance that appears anytime in the first year is what we call "splitting." Splitting involves the client's setting up her mentors in opposition to one another so that she does not have to take responsibility for her unhealthy behavior. The client is essentially playing one counselor against another. This is especially common in addictions (whether to food or chemicals) in which clients tend to be involved with more than one helping system. For example, the client may have a primary counselor, a different counselor as group leader, a counselor for each of her children involved in the Department of Social Services system, and a medical professional who advocates the use of medication as a "cure" for the addiction.

The client splits these authorities by distorting or misrepresenting to one professional what another professional is saying about the client's treatment. This allows the client to feel special and powerful while not taking responsibility for her treatment. This behavior harks back to playing one parent against another in order to feel special and is also a continuation of a lifelong technique of avoiding responsibility by blaming flawed (nonperfect) authorities.

Splitting is extremely common, as well as aggravating, in inpatient treatment programs in which the client works with several counselors and also goes to outside meetings. The client will disagree with what you are saying by quoting another staff member who has expressed a belief contrary to ours. Or the client will attempt to be special or privileged by showing other clients and staff how his relationship with you is somehow more special than theirs.

Splitting is best dealt with by the professionals together confronting the client. Of course, if the staff members *are* playing favorites or if they side with the splitting client without checking out the client's claims with the staff first, then they are as unhealthy as the client, and the client's unhealthy behavior cannot be worked through. The client learns nothing about her behavior and may even be discharged from an inpatient facility for this form of resistance if the staff becomes too overwhelmed. Before taking as truth what our client says about another professional, we should "consider the source," as we say, the source being the patient or client. We need to check with the other professionals involved.

A form of splitting may also occur between you and A.A. members or sponsors, especially if you are not in recovery yourself. The client may passively attack you by quoting something she heard in A.A, for instance, that counseling or psychotherapy is not a good thing, or that "civilians" just can't understand the disease. Or the client may begin to distance himself from the program by "hearing what he wants to hear," which generally involves taking things out of context. He sets us up against the program and then tries to gain our alliance against the program.

To deal with this manipulation, we can picture the client as an angry child who does not want to do chores. He is standing in the middle of two parents who cannot agree on child rearing and who are also angry at each other. Addicted clients, generally, are also codependent, and they are very good at tuning into our vulnerabilities and fears and using these as a way to avoid taking responsibility. The client gets the two parents fighting and then slips out to do what he wants to do. If the parents later confront him on his failure to do his chores, whom can they hold accountable? Let's not get caught up in debating whose approach to sobriety is the better one. Given the number of active addicts, it's clear that no one has found "the cure." I also remind my clients that even Bill W. (a founder of A.A.) was in psychotherapy.

Stage V:
Intimacy Development Specific to Recovery

Intimacy in Stage V has to do with developing and maintaining friendships, not the intimacy of romantic or sexual relationships. The psychosocial crisis for this stage is intimacy versus isolation. The potential strengths are love versus exclusivity. The resolution of this stage typically occurs during years two and three. The recovering person needs to learn how to get her social needs met. Relationships are very difficult for recovering persons in general. They struggle with issues of control and assertiveness. They often ask whether they should voice their feelings about something or whether they should hold back and let it pass. This stage is very important because it is when the client generally begins to get in touch with "old" feelings of abandonment, betrayal, and shame. How our client deals with these feelings can make or break his recovery.

The most important aspects in this stage are the spiritual and the relational/emotional. The client's faith is really put to the test. Although the client may say that he has faith in a higher power, when it comes to relationships this faith is tested. Many clients will sell their faith short in order to have the relationship they want regardless of whether it is good for their recovery. This is particularly true if they feel they are in love with this other person. Clients have the opportunity to work on honesty and trust. They have let go of the need to control drugs and alcohol; now they need to let go of the need to control others. This is a very difficult challenge.

Stage V Tasks

There is a broad range of tasks that may be included in the intimacy stage of recovery. The client is working on maintaining his recovery program and, at this same time, moving on to incorporate more of life's experiences into his program of recovery. Tasks for this stage include relapse prevention work, in which we help the client identify situations that threaten her sobriety. The assumption behind relapse prevention is that there are clear warning signs that the client is going to drink or use drugs months prior to his actually doing so. Warning signs may be in the form of behavior (missing meetings), attitude (resentment, self-pity), or feelings (anger, depression, sadness, fear). Often clues to the client's triggers can be gained from his past slips and relapses. We help the client write out the beliefs and feelings involved in high-risk situations. We teach the client how to avoid these situations or, if he finds himself in a high-risk situation, how to cope without resorting to taking a drink or a drug. The client learns to identify the warning signs of his "budding" (building up to drink) and what to do about it when he is aware of these signs. There are many resources available on relapse prevention (e.g., Maultsby, 1978).

In addition to identifying and watching for the warning signs of relapse, the client is taking steps to further her involvement in recovery. She does this by joining a self-help group and a Step group, and going on speaking engagements or "commitments" with her group. She may begin to go on A.A. retreats or conventions. She is working on being honest with herself and others through her counseling and support groups. She is socializing with friends, family, and relatives, and she is beginning to identify her codependent behaviors as she does so.

Resistance and Solutions in Stage V

Much of the work during this stage has to do with exploring how clients feel about the way they are treated by others. Clients seem very angry, and in time they come to see that beneath this anger often lies hurt. This stage involves asking the clients questions about how they felt when their friend, spouse, or child said what they did or treated them the way they did and why they felt this way. Relationships are a way for the client to get in touch with beliefs and feelings he has previously denied. For example, our client may deny that he seeks others' approval but that assertion is tested in relationships. He sees in relationships that he really does deny his true feelings in order to be liked by other people. We continue to work on identifying and challenging irrational beliefs and feelings.

Issues of codependence become more obvious at this stage of recovery. Clients take responsibility for others' feelings and place them above their own. They may begin to agree to sponsor too many people or they may begin counseling other people in a halfway house in their free time. They may begin going to their spouse's meetings or criticizing their spouse's recovery. They are angry at their sponsor (and often their counselor) for not being able to help them. In short, they may begin spending all their time, energy, and finances helping others' sobriety while neglecting their own. They begin to feel guilt-ridden and angry and overwhelmed as the boundaries between themselves and others crumble.

We need to help clients set limits on their caretaking. For instance, clients may cut back on or stop sponsoring people. We may also begin to explore their role in their family of origin. Possibly they were the caretaker in the family, and the only way they know how to connect with others is by taking care of them. They feel good about themselves only when they are needed by others. We are only just beginning to look to their childhood. We are beginning to ask how a present behavior relates to their role in their family of origin. We are setting the stage for the clients to connect their childhood experiences with their present unresolved conflicts.

Up to this point, we have dealt with inappropriate feelings by challenging the belief system. That is, we may challenge the belief that the boss *should* always be fair. Now we are saying, "I wonder where those beliefs came from. I wonder how fair your parents were in the treatment of you and your siblings?" Now that the client has some way of coping with her feelings, we encourage her to get in touch with her feelings and "sit with them," i.e., feel and process through these feelings. The client is preparing to move on to the next stage, which involves getting back in touch with the self she lost so long ago and learning about her needs as separate from the needs of others.

STAGES VI AND VII

Identity and Intimacy Development

Stage VI: Identity Development

In Stage VI, the internal and external structures we have set up with our client are working and the client is maintaining sobriety. The client has achieved some measure of safety in sobriety. As long as the client does not neglect his recovery plan, he can now begin to explore additional aspects of self. This stage relates, then, to a more general knowledge about self rather than a self only in relation to sobriety. The crisis is the same: identity versus identity confusion with the emerging strength of fidelity versus repudiation. The resolution of this stage generally takes place during years three through five. The counseling or therapy in Stage VI is not much different from counseling an individual who is not in recovery. Counselors who are trained to deal only with addiction may want to consider referring the client to a more generally trained counselor at this point, depending on the issue at hand and level of competence in handling that issue.

Several issues do occur more often in the recovering client. Most likely, the person came from a dysfunctional home with one or two alcoholic parents. There are issues such as abuse and neglect. We need to explore the role our client played in this dysfunctional system. Working through the impact of dysfunctional parents on the client is important because very often these clients have not separated from this system. On the roles adult children play in their family of origin, I recommend Claudia Black (1981) and John Bradshaw (1988).

The client needs to separate psychologically from the family system of origin if it continues to be an unhealthy one, in order to be free of his compulsion. Because the system is sick, it is our client and not the sick family system who must set limits. Often the client is drawn back into the system out of guilt and shame. For example, if our client always played the scapegoat, she continues to be every member's excuse for the problems in their lives. They do not want our client to escape this role because then they would have to look at themselves. We must help our client see that she needs to give up this identity as a scapegoat, and part of doing so is letting go of the sick family system that continues to reinforce this negative identity.

Separating from unhealthy loved ones brings up feelings of loss, and these feelings connect back to childhood losses. We begin to discuss losses that result from being brought up in a dysfunctional home. The client missed out on having a healthy parent-child relationship. Often the client was an addict through junior high and high school and missed out on that part of her life as well. Kübler-Ross's book *On Death and Dying* (1969) is helpful in identifying where the client is in the process of grieving these losses.

Until the client is free of his sick family, it is very difficult for him not to bring this sickness into his next intimate relationship or his own family system. At first this process is only intellectual. Later on, the client becomes aware of the continuing impact of his family of origin on his present relationships. He then begins to have feelings about his family of origin.

Issues of codependence continue to be dealt with in this stage. The client begins to explore how she defines herself in relation to others, e.g., as a mother, a wife, a career person, a daughter. We need to find the answers to the following questions: Where does this client get her self-esteem? What are her strengths? Does she have a view of herself separate from those she takes care of, or is defined by? Or, alternatively, does she continue to live a role-defined existence with no awareness of boundaries between self and others? Codependence, in my opinion, is more a problem of identity and individuation than a problem of intimacy. The person continues to define herself through others and has her needs met through taking care of others. In working on this, we focus not on the relationship but on what the client is avoiding within herself.

Three Aspects of Self

The emotional/relational aspect comes to the fore, as does the spiritual. At this point, the approach shifts somewhat from a cognitive approach to a more emotional approach. Bradshaw's books and exercises are very helpful in working through feelings about ourselves and the roles we played in our family of origin and continue to play in our relationships today. Many clients are not in touch with their inner child. Getting the client to pay attention to the child within helps her focus on her needs and not on the needs of the family of origin or her new intimate relationships.

The spiritual aspect shows itself in the client's willingness to move beyond a focus on how not to use the addictive substance to how to grow and realize his potential. As they say, this requires a "leap of faith" similar to the leap of faith required in giving up dependence on a substance. Now the person is asked to give up much of what he knows to be his identity. This identity may be negative but it is all he has. The client is now saying, "I am more than just an alcoholic; I am also a human being with all sorts of strengths and weaknesses, and I need to begin identifying those."

Another issue is giving up other obsessive-compulsive behaviors such as smoking or overeating. Clients will generally bring up the desire to give up these other compulsions themselves. They need to approach these compulsions in the same way they approached chemical dependence, the obvious difference being that they do not necessarily abstain from these other compulsions. For instance, in a food addiction the client needs to begin to pay attention to her internal cues (thoughts, feelings) when she begins to overeat.

Another issue specific to chemical dependence is a delayed adolescence. If our client has a long history of drinking or drugging, then he is probably developmentally delayed. For example, a thirty-year-old may only be at the adolescent stage of psychosocial development because of the interrupting effects of alcohol or drugs. So it is appropriate that he is having an identity crisis and is trying to find himself in his relationships with others, especially adolescent love and sexual relationships. The goal at this point is to help him keep from losing himself, his identity as a separate individual in these relationships, and to support him in his search for a new identity.

Often clients in the third and fourth years begin to get down on themselves for not being age-appropriate. They say things like, "I'm thirty years old. I should be married with kids now, not asking who I am!" We need to point out the developmental periods that they missed and the need for them to take their time in finding out who they are and what they want and need.

Clients often begin to question their careers at this stage. Many will return to school to further themselves in their present field or to change fields or to find out what school is like without being high on alcohol or drugs. This can be a very healthy experience that boosts self-image and self-esteem as the client realizes that she has not lost her capacity to think, and that she can make it in school without the aid of drugs. For others, returning to school is necessary because they have lost their means of support. They may have lost their financial support because they supported themselves by the selling of drugs, because they have left a dangerous living situation where they were supported by a partner, or because they cannot return to their old career (their license has been revoked or the risk is too great).

Stage VI Tasks

Identity development tasks include all that the client needs to do in order to find out more about himself. In order to further focus on himself, he works on giving up his remaining addictions: food, smoking, workaholism, codependent behavior. He identifies and deals with family-of-origin issues: adult child of an alcoholic issues, sexual abuse, and so on. He learns to identify the role he played in the family and how he has continued to play out this role in his life today. He learns to stop doing that. It is no longer okay for him to be the scapegoat in his family of origin or in his workplace. He is able to identify and accept his strengths and weaknesses. He begins to question his satisfaction with his career and education and looks to adjust these areas to find a better fit with his new knowledge about self. He may return to school to finish a degree or begin to look for a job that better suits his needs.

Resistance and Solutions in Stage VI

Clients often resist moving forward to this stage out of fear of failure. They have found some safety in defining themselves as "recovering alcoholics," and now we are asking them to expand on their identities. Resistance comes in several forms. They may return to their addictive behavior, they may develop other compulsions or defiant behavior, or they may become stuck at a self-focused or role-focused level of development. Clients will resist this stage by regressing to other forms of dependency. Sometimes they will even verbalize their resistance by saying things like, "I'm not as healthy as you think I am!" Many people do not positively resolve this stage. They may stay rigidly stuck, but they do not necessarily return to their addictive behavior.

Within these psychosocial stages of identity and intimacy are developmental levels, including self-focused, role-focused, and individuated-connected levels. In the intimacy measure presented in the next stage, there is a "conventional" or "role-defined" level of intimacy in which the majority of all people, not just those in recovery, get stuck. There is also a role-defined level of identity. Simply put, people stop asking questions about their existence and simply work with what they have. They lack awareness of their internal selves. People in recovery have achieved a "role-defined" identity in the form of "I am a recovering alcoholic," and they do not necessarily move beyond that stage.

When a client does not positively resolve this stage by integrating other identity components into her image of self, often what we see is a juvenile cliquishness. This is evident when A.A. is used as a social club and, like all social clubs, it functions partly so that the few who belong can exclude the many who do not. The behavior of these cliques is not much different from what we all experienced in high school. The focus is on the external self: compulsively buying the right clothes, exercising at the right fitness clubs, going to the right vacation resorts. Improved outward appearance is a positive indicator of recovery, but it needs to reflect an improved self-image, not substitute for it.

One danger of staying at a role-focused level is that often negative identity elements are also present, representing the anger or defiance that the client has not worked through. For example, one client of mine knew the lingo of the program inside and out. She was educated and successful, and she had recently married a recovering addict who was now also successful. But she could not give up the control necessary to move on developmentally. She was hooked on an addictive lifestyle even though she was no longer using chemicals. She held onto her control (and fears and anger) by resuming her cigarette smoking and by being codependently involved with nonrecovering addicts. She continues to live two lives: the perfect girl in recovery and the bad girl acting out her defiance. She has not yet taken the "leap of faith" needed to give up her compulsions and look at the void that is within herself.

There is a certain blindness or lack of awareness in people at the role-focused and self-focused levels. For those in recovery, they continue to "work the program," but it is an intellectual and not an emotional exercise. Can people in recovery stay at these identity levels and stay sober? Although we do not want to judge the quality of people's recovery, I think the term "dry drunk" appropriately describes many people who do not positively resolve the identity and intimacy stages of development. They can continue to live addiction-free, but sobriety is much more than not using the substance. Persons who are stuck at these levels are similar to the dry drunk in that they fail to take a good look at themselves and work to give up defenses that keep them from freely accepting and loving themselves and others. I think this difference becomes even more apparent as the individual attempts to have intimate sexual and romantic relationships.

How can we deal with this failure to move positively on to the next stage? Not very easily, because there is nothing very obviously wrong. There is no concrete problem. Look how bad it had to get before our clients did something about a behavior that was killing them! Addicts are used to feeling so bad that feeling relatively good becomes "good enough" or, as we say in the addiction field, they think "better is healthy." If people return to a compulsive behavior, we can work on that because it is tangible. But if people simply do not want to work on moving forward to gain greater feelings of self-acceptance, there is little more we can do. This is a good time to temporarily suspend treatment so that the client can test out her new behaviors and see what she feels is missing.

People find it very difficult to imagine a developmental stage beyond the one they are in. Sometimes we can involve clients in change if their spouse or lover is threatening to leave them, but this too is tricky because they often blame the spouse and deny that they are part of the problem. Moreover, the problem is not yet an issue of couples therapy; it is an issue for individual or group therapy. We wind up with a couples issue because the recovering individual denies it is his problem. Until the client works through this identity stage, he will not achieve self-acceptance nor will he find the "mature love" promised in the next stage. The intimacy stage will find a negative resolution in the form of isolation or codependence.

Stage VII: Intimacy in Love Relationships

Like in the previous stage, counseling the client in this stage is not very different from counseling a nonrecovering individual with an intimacy problem. The psychosocial crisis of this stage is intimacy versus isolation. The strength to emerge from the positive resolution of this stage is mature love. The resolution of this stage often occurs during years three through five. A discussion of how to help clients develop intimate relationships is beyond the scope of this book. However, I hope to provide an idea of how to assess and talk about the client's level of intimacy within relationships.

Some issues show up more often in recovering clients. Often childhood sexual abuse will appear at this point. The client may have been acting out sexually her whole life as a way of not getting close to another person. When she stops acting out sexually and stops using drugs and alcohol to not feel, she begins to recall the childhood sexual abuse. Once she works through her feelings about this abuse, her capacity for intimacy increases.

Another problem arises when a client was married prior to getting sober and is married to the same person now in sobriety. The spouse married a dysfunctional person (our client), which practically guaranteed there would be no intimacy. The spouse, then, has his own issues with intimacy, and if he does not work on them along with his wife, then the relationship is not going to be intimate. This is extremely frustrating for the client who is working hard to have an intimate relationship. She can do one of three things: accept that she is not going to experience intimacy, wait and hope that the spouse will change, or get out of the marriage. Our client can learn to detach herself from a spouse who causes her pain, through counseling and self-help groups (e.g., Al-Anon), but detachment is not intimacy. She is still left with a nonintimate relationship.

New intimate relationships are somewhat easier to negotiate. Our client has worked on herself and is now ready to find a partner who is as committed to intimacy as he is. Now that the person has a better-developed sense of self, she is less likely to be attracted to an unhealthy person. And because she has become healthier, she is also less likely to attract an unhealthy person.

How can we help our clients move on and positively resolve this final stage? Again, it is never easy and it is sometimes not possible. Since intimacy is itself a vague term, we need to begin by concretely defining intimacy and by asking the client about his feelings concerning the quality of his relationships. Most of our clients will say they don't even know what love is, to say nothing of the concept of intimacy. Another common problem is that they have for so long been the caretakers in relationships, they do not even know what to ask for in terms of intimacy. Many are from broken or dysfunctional homes so there was no modeling of intimacy. They do not have a standard against which to measure the intimacy of their relationships. In helping to educate ourselves and the client regarding intimate and nonintimate behaviors, a useful tool is the scale of intimacy developed by White (1989) and described as follows.

Intimacy Scale

According to this measure, components of an intimate relationship include: orientation, caring/concern, sexuality (relevant only for sexually intimate relationships), commitment, and communication/openness. These components are assessed through an open-ended interview (appendix D, p. 175) and the responses are then categorized according to level. This interview can help identify the level of functioning of a long-term relationship and can also help identify an addictive new relationship. Evaluating the intimacy in a relationship is also helpful for partners who are considering getting married or for married partners who are considering having children.

Each component is scored individually on developmental scales ranging from a low stage 1 to a high stage 6. The six stages can be grouped into three developmental levels: low, medium, and high, and these levels are labeled self-focused, role-focused, and individuated-connected. One important assumption is that one's level of maturity may differ across relationships. For instance, a client may have a more mature relationship with one person (e.g., a spouse) than with another (e.g., a same-sex friend).

Level 1: Self-focused

The individual at this level sees the partner as a means to a selfish ends or as an obstacle to those ends. Descriptions of the other are as a source of supply or as a hostile rival for supplies. At this level there is no acknowledgment of the other's equality or separateness, little or no concept of the other's views or feelings. Descriptions of the relationship focus on the subject's own needs (which may be described in glowing detail) and on the partner's success or failure in meeting those needs, but not on the processes internal to the relationship. For some clients at this level, the quality of description may indicate a paucity of inner experience and a feeling of interior emptiness. Extreme dependency on the other, which may take a hostile form, is one possible manifestation of a Level 1 relationship.

Level 2: Role-focused

At this intermediate level individuals have a basic understanding that the other has needs and feelings too, but their descriptions of relationships lack complexity and depth. Responses tend to focus on concrete, external things as the source of problems or as the way to express support. For example: "The only thing I'd like to change in the relationship is to have a better work schedule and be making more money," or "I hug him and kiss him and make sure his dinner is cooked and he has clean clothes to wear to work." "He pays the bills and makes sure the car is running."

Descriptions of the relationship take on the form of stereotyped images of a happy marriage. They are socially acceptable responses, lacking in specific examples that demonstrate an appreciation of the partner's individuality. Role-focused responses lack introspection, and there is a tendency to generalize. The role-focused individual lacks an imaginative, intuitive sense of what it is like to be inside the other's skin. That person needs to have the partner's needs or feelings spelled out. For example: "I used to get upset about how bitchy she was when I came home from work, but she explained to me how ragged she gets after being with the kids all day, and now I try to take that into account." Many relationships at this level are comfortable and happy, with both partners carrying out roles that society expects from good citizens.

The role-focused level of intimacy describes the type discussed in Stage V, intimacy specific to sobriety. Most of our client's relationships with other A.A. members are role-focused in that they are limited to, or defined by, the A.A. setting and program and do not extend beyond that role. As with marital relationships, these may be happy and comfortable, but they are limited because they are role-defined, e.g., the only bond in the relationship may be sobriety. Intimate relationships with the opposite sex (spouse, lover) may also be role-defined and this gets in the way of appreciating and facilitating each other's development. The spouse may not complain about, and may even encourage, her recovering spouse to attend more meetings, but she is threatened by those behaviors that do not conform to her concept of recovery. For example, she may get angry at her spouse for his meditation routine because it excludes her and because she does not value that element of recovery.

Level 3: Individuated-Connected

Intimate behavior goes beyond a stereotyped, socially acceptable format, with a resulting depth of connection. A mature ability to cope with disappointment, tolerate struggle, and make compromises must be evident. An answer that convincingly demonstrates that conflicts in the relationship are faced and dealt with, and goes on to express satisfaction and even joy in the partnership, would qualify as highly intimate. There must be evidence that a free choice is made to be close with the specific partner, a choice made from a position of autonomy rather than out of need or convenience. The client should demonstrate the ability to recognize the partner's individuality, to appreciate the other's unique qualities, and to take pleasure in enhancing the development of the other's talents and powers.

At this level, clients refer to more than the concrete, visible signs of the relationship's quality. They have a concern with the emotional and even spiritual satisfaction to be gained from intimacy with this particular partner. They demonstrate a willingness to pay a lot of attention to "our relationship" and how it is going.

Stage VII Tasks

This stage of intimacy is more about relationship process than about recovery tasks. The client is maintaining her recovery program and is vigilant regarding the possibility of developing substitute addictions. She is learning what her needs are and how to have those needs met in intimate relationships. She is learning how to give up old unhealthy relationships and how to choose new healthy partners. She is working on accepting nonperfection in others and in herself in relation to others. She is working on being less self-focused and is learning how to take the perspective of another (put herself in the other's shoes) in order that she develop *a mutual* relationship in which both partners can have their needs met.

Resistance and Solutions in Stage VII

Like in the prior stage of identity development, there is little we do to facilitate a person's development of intimacy if he does not identify it as a problem. If our client identifies it as a problem but his spouse does not and the spouse is not willing to work on the relationship, then there is little our client can do other than accept the relationship, hope for a change in the future, or give up the relationship in hopes of finding a more intimate partner. If it is our client who does not want to work on intimacy (but her partner does) then there is little more we can do than help her get in touch with her feelings about their relationship, for example, her feelings about her partner's dissatisfaction with the relationship. Couples counseling or therapy would be a good referral for a client and spouse who are willing to work on achieving intimacy in their relationship.

In my experience I do not find that a lack of mature love necessarily leads the client back to the use of a chemical, although the client does tend to go through phases of addictive behaviors: food, nicotine, sex. Her ability to "settle" for "less" in a relationship is no different from the nonrecovering person's tendency to do so. This level is called role-focused or conventional because it is just that: the norm that most people in our society develop to, but not beyond.

What I see happening typically is that the recovering person attempts to positively resolve this stage. She then finds it either too threatening to give up the necessary amount of control or finds a partner unwilling or unavailable. She then refocuses to self and identity development in the form of furthering her education and career (or those of her children). This development is less threatening because it is something she can do on her own and does not need to put her feelings on the line to achieve success. In terms of relationships, the person continues to be self-focused, codependent, and emotionally isolated. On the positive side, there is always the possibility that, in time, the client will feel safe enough to take the risks needed to move on to a positive resolution of the intimacy stage.

WHAT IS RECOVERY?

What is recovery? In the first edition of this book I attempted to sum up what recovery meant to me as a professional working in the field. I wrote that recovery meant health, giving up the sick role. Being healthy means taking responsibility for our life, being curious and creative, moving forward positively to discover new things, enjoying ourselves in the moment, loving and being loved, and experiencing acceptance of self and others. That all still fits with my concept of recovery. I would add to that a spiritual aspect. I think it is believing in a power greater than ourselves, be that God, or children, or love. I think it is having at the same time both a sense of peace and the desire to move forward and discover new things without allowing fear of failure to stop us. My definition of recovery applies to what everyone, not just people "in recovery," seek from life.

This time around, I decided to ask some other people who I know have "it" for their definitions of recovery. Here are some of the responses I received:

—

Recovery to me is getting back my life, free from the bondage of alcoholism and addiction. In my case, it was done by learning how to live through the twelve steps of A.A. It is a process of dealing with the disease that is threefold: physical, mental, and spiritual.

In practicing the principles I learned from A.A. in combination with therapeutic counseling I strive to be a better person and can deal with the ups and downs of everyday life without picking up a drink or a drug to escape the way I cope with them. It is an ongoing process and I simply practice these principles every day. One day at a time.

— T. P.

—

I am not 100 percent married to "recovery" as an expression of where I am in my life's journey. I think I prefer to name the recovery work I do as the crust of the pie of my life. Prior to recovery I had no life, and in early recovery it was vital to breathe, eat, and live as much of recovery as possible. Today, life is more about living and making the right choices that create peace, love, joy, and serenity in all my relationships. It is so much about showing up to responsibilities, taking care of myself so that I can continue to show up and practicing kindness in all that I do. This does not always happen, and that is where my "recovery" work continues. When I find myself in a place of pain, unrest, resentment, it is vital for me to explore what actions or faulty beliefs brought me there, forgive myself, learn the lesson, let it go, and keep living. This way of life would crumble without my relationship with God. God is the source of it all. Practicing forgiveness is the way.

— M. M. C.

—

Recovery has given me the freedom to choose. I was lost in the world of alcohol and other drugs and couldn't see how much I had hurt the ones I loved. I have found a new way to live, through the Twelve Steps and a God of my own understanding. The obsession to use has been lifted. I have found the gift of daily help, and all I have to do is tap into that source of power. Recovery has given me true friends today, none like I have ever had before. They have one goal in mind and that is to help me stay clean and sober. I can never say thank you too much for the gift of sobriety.

— H. R. M. Sr.

—

Recovery is a lifelong bidding to recapture the splendor that a life once had. This invitation is sent to the darkest place in one's soul — a place where guilt, shame, and loneliness have crept in to reside. Upon one's admitting to God and another human being this dim dwelling and sense of hopelessness, a pinhole of light pierces that soul and there is cast a faint view of Promise. Cleansing rays light the path as we then turn to the care of a loving God, humbly letting him guide and empower us. Acknowledging wrongs done, healing that comes with making amends, and daily prayer burn a light so bright that others who see it might be drawn out of their own addicted darkness into this luminescence that God has for us all.

—*J. G.*

THE TWELVE STEPS OF ALCOHOLICS ANONYMOUS

1. We admitted we were powerless over alcohol—that our lives had become unmanageable.

2. Came to believe that a Power greater than ourselves could restore us to sanity.

3. Made a decision to turn our will and our lives over to the care of God *as we understood Him.*

4. Made a searching and fearless moral inventory of ourselves.

5. Admitted to God, to ourselves, and to another human being the exact nature of our wrongs.

6. Were entirely ready to have God remove all these defects of character.

7. Humbly asked Him to remove our shortcomings.

8. Made a list of all persons we had harmed, and became willing to make amends to them all.

9. Made direct amends to such people wherever possible, except when to do so would injure them or others.

10. Continued to take personal inventory and when we were wrong promptly admitted it.

11. Sought through prayer and meditation to improve our conscious contact with God, *as we understood Him*, praying only for knowledge of His will for us and the power to carry that out.

12. Having had a spiritual awakening as the result of these steps, we tried to carry this message to alcoholics, and to practice these principles in all our affairs.

The Twelve Steps are reprinted with permission of Alcoholics Anonymous World Services, Inc. Permission to reprint the Twelve Steps does not mean that A.A. has reviewed or approved the contents of this publication nor that A.A. agrees with the views expressed herein. A.A. is a program of recovery from alcoholism — use of the Twelve Steps in connection with programs and activities which are patterned after A.A., but which address other problems, does not imply otherwise.

SAMPLE
TREATMENT PLANS

Inpatient

Problem 1:	Chemical dependency
Objective (goal):	Sobriety maintenance
Method:	1. No use of alcohol/drugs 2. Attend A.A./N.A.
Objective (goal):	Understand disease of addiction

Method:	1. Psychoeducation: read Steps 1, 2, 3 and "Merry-Go-Round"
	2. Assess knowledge of biological/psychological components of alcohol
	3. Learn to access A.A. and understand program:
	   a. Obtain telephone numbers
	   b. Obtain temporary sponsor

Objective (goal):	Understand addiction as pertains to self

Method:	1. Written assignments
	   a. Good-bye letter to drug/alcohol
	   b. Life-o-gram
	   c. Collage
	   d. Daily structure log
	2. Increase verbalization/participation in peer group, recovery plan developed
	3. Identify high-risk situations, craving triggers
	4. Identify path of progression leading to present admission

Objective (goal):	Decrease denial
Method:	Increase participation in peer group Elicit feedback from group members Meet 1 : 1 with each of other residents
Problem 2:	Decreased capacity to cope with stress
Objective (goal):	Learn tolerance of uncomfortable feelings
Method:	1. Develop relaxation skills/relaxation exercises 2. Use guided imagery 3. Write in a journal 4. Seek out others to talk through uncomfortable feelings 5. Identify sources of stress and coping capacity

Outpatient

Individual Treatment Plan (First Three Months in Treatment)

Problem 1:   Chemical dependency

Date identified _____ Date resolved _____
Expected achievement date _____ Date achieved _____

Objective 1:	Sobriety maintenance: a practical view
Method(s):	Attend A.A./N.A. 3X/week (ongoing) Join a group (target time: one month) Get and utilize a sponsor (target time: one month) Individual and group therapy (ongoing)
Objective 2:	Sober environment at home
Method(s):	Either have husband move out or have client find a sober house or apartment with sober roommate (target time: prearranged for discharge date)
Objective 3:	Develop return-to-work agreement
Method(s):	Return-to-work agreement (with restrictions) to be signed by client, employer, and counselor Follow-through with contract conditions (target time: one to three months)

Was the client involved in the incorporation of this problem in the treatment plan? Yes ___ No ___ Explain: _____

_____

Staff member: _____ Client: _____

Individual Treatment Plan (Three to Six Months)

Problem 1:   Chemical dependency

Date identified _____ Date resolved _____
Expected achievement date _____ Date achieved _____

Objective 1:   Sobriety maintenance

Method(s):   No change, continue with plan: A.A./N.A., individual, group

Objective 2:   Increase socialization/leisure-time activity

Method(s):   Introduce self to two new members at each meeting and get
                 phone numbers
                 Ask someone out for coffee (same-sex)
                 Go to a movie with a friend

Objective 3:   Building trustworthy relationships

Method(s):   Take a risk in group counseling by sharing something you find
                 difficult to accept about yourself
                 Give someone in the group feedback about your feelings
                 toward them

Was the client involved in the incorporation of this problem in the treatment
plan? Yes ___ No ___ Explain: _____
_____

Staff member: _____ Client: _____

Individual Treatment Plan (Six to Twelve Months)

Problem 1:   Chemical dependency

Date identified _____ Date resolved _____
Expected achievement date _____ Date achieved _____

Objective 1:   Sobriety maintenance

Method(s):   Utilize sponsor more often
                 Express anger toward sponsor
                 If conflict not resolvable, find new sponsor and discuss issues
                 with old sponsor

Objective 2:   Resolve marital problems

Method(s):   If husband does not have a plan for getting sober, discuss
                 separation (emotional) from husband

Objective 3:   Identifying and expressing feelings

Method(s):   Discuss individually and then in a group situation where you
                felt shame (versus guilt)
                Let someone close to you know when he hurt you

Objective 4:   Discuss client's level of comfort at work and consider reducing
                restrictions or taking a leave of absence

Was the client involved in the incorporation of this problem in the treatment
plan? Yes ___ No ___ Explain: _____

_____

Staff member: _____ Client: _____

Individual Treatment Plan (Year Two)
Problem 1:   Chemical dependency

Date identified _____ Date resolved _____
Expected achievement date _____ Date achieved _____

Objective 1:   Continue with sobriety maintenance plan

Objective 2:   Continue to work on marital issues

Method(s):   Discuss effects of emotional and physical abuse by husband on
                self-esteem
                Discuss feelings of helplessness and hopelessness
                Possible grieving of lost relationship with husband (if husband
                sober, discuss couples counseling)

Objective 3:   Continue to work on self-esteem

Method(s):   Further development of relationships
                Possible return for further education, getting self in shape
                physically, pursuing a hobby, taking art classes, etc.
                Identifying and speaking up for her rights, e.g., assertiveness
                with boss

Objective 4:   Begin to discuss adult child and sexual abuse issues

Method(s):   Discuss in individual and then group counseling
                Go to ACOA meeting
                Learn to identify codependent behavior

Objective 5:   Begin to discuss relapse plan and termination issues

Was the client involved in the incorporation of this problem in the treatment
plan? Yes ___ No ___ Explain: _____

_____

Staff member: _____ Client: _____

RETURN-TO-WORK AGREEMENT between
_____ and _____

The following is a review of the conditions for my return to work as discussed in our meeting of _____.

1. I will remain drug and alcohol free.

2. I will continue active treatment at Lexington Recovery Associates (LRA).

3. LRA will do an ongoing assessment of my progress in rehabilitation, as well as urine screens.

4. If it has been determined that I am in relapse, LRA will inform:
   _____.

5. I give general permission for _____ to contact LRA if s(he) suspects any abuse. LRA staff will do an assessment of my status and notify _____ of any findings.

6. I will maintain contact with _____ for the purpose of support and assessment. I give permission for random urine screens to be called for by _____.

7. A copy of this agreement will be held by _____.

The date of _____ is established as my reentry date at _____ on a full-time/part-time (day/week) schedule. On _____ it will be determined by LRA and

_____ as to an increase in hours worked per week.

No access to or administration of addictive drugs is permitted at this time. Re-instatement of medication passing privileges will be determined by LRA and

_____ .

It is also understood that I will be working eight-hour shifts and I will not be working alone.

If I do not follow the above expectations or have any serious job performance difficulties, disciplinary action may occur.

Comments: _____

_____

I have read and understand this agreement and freely give my consent to its implementation.

This agreement will automatically expire: _____ .

_____   _____   _____
LRA representative   Employer   Client

= Appendix D =

INTIMACY MATURITY
INTERVIEW

The following intimacy maturity interview is the male form, for those married or living with someone. The form for females and forms for males and females not involved with a member of the opposite sex, as well as the scoring manual for the Intimacy Scale, can be obtained by writing to: Kathleen M. White, Ed.D., Boston University, Department of Psychology, 64 Cummington Street, Boston, MA 02215.

I have included this form because I find that many people, including professional helpers, do not know how to talk with clients about intimacy. They do not possess a language of intimacy and, therefore, do not know what to look for in helping clients assess intimacy in their relationships. Developing the capacity for intimacy within a person and within a relationship appears to be the most difficult challenge of later recovery. Having a means of communicating with the client about intimacy is a beginning to facilitating its development.

Intimacy Maturity Interview
(Male: married or living with someone)

Basically we're interested in learning about people's closest relationships with members of the same and opposite sex. Let's start with the relationship you consider to be your closest.

Who would this be? How long have you been close? Would you briefly describe this person? What is she like? What is her view of you?

What kinds of activities do the two of you do separately? (yourself) (her)

How do you feel when your wife (girlfriend) gets involved in outside or separate activities? Why?

How does your wife (girlfriend) feel when you get involved in outside or separate activities? Why?

Do you mind it when your wife (girlfriend) takes on new activities or interests? Why?

Does your wife (girlfriend) mind it when you take on new activities or interests? Why?

What kinds of things do the two of you usually talk about together? (Do you share worries and problems?)

Do you talk about your relationship with one another? What things concerning your relationship do you talk about?

Do you share problems or differences within the relationship?

(If interviewee says we don't have problems, use optional probes) How are these dealt with? Why this way?

Who usually initiates efforts to deal with such problems? If unequal, why?

How do you react when she brings up problems or concerns to you about your relationship? Why?

How does she react when you bring up problems or concerns to her about your relationship? Why?

Are there any ways in which you could be more open with her? Are there any ways in which she could be more open with you?

Optional Probes for the above section on disclosure and communication.

People sometimes get on each other's nerves in some way or another. Is there anything about your wife (girlfriend) that you dislike? Have you discussed this with her?

Is there anything about yourself that gets on your wife's (girlfriend's) nerves? Has she expressed this to you?

Do you ever have any fights? How do they usually get started? How do the two of you deal with such differences?

What ways do you show your wife (girlfriend) you care about her?

Would she like you to express your caring differently?

What ways does your wife (girlfriend) show she cares about you?

Would you like her to express her caring differently?

(Do you do things for each other without being asked or go out of your way to help?)

Would your wife (girlfriend) say you are as concerned about her needs as your own? If no, why?

In regards to the sexual side of the relationship, are you satisfied with the way things are?

Is your wife (girlfriend) satisfied with the sexual side of your relationship?

As a couple, have you discussed the sexual aspect of your relationship with each other? Explain.

How frequently do you have such discussions?

Would you like to see anything change? Explain.

How do you think she would view these changes?

Would your wife (girlfriend) like to see any changes? Explain.

What do you think of these changes?

Overall, have there been any important changes in your sexual relations?

How have you reacted to these changes?

How has she?

In reference to your relationship overall, does one of you show more involvement than the other? If yes, why is this so and is this a source of difficulties?

How committed to this relation are you? Your wife (girlfriend)?

Do you ever feel in conflict about this relationship?

Do you ever think about alternatives to your present relationship?

Given that every relation has room to grow, how could you contribute to improving the general quality of your relationship as it currently exists?

REFERENCES AND BIBLIOGRAPHY

Adams, I. B., and B. R. Martin. 1996. "Cannabis: Pharmacology and Toxicology in Animals and Humans." *Addiction* 91: 1585–1614.

Alcoholics Anonymous. 1985. *Alcoholics Anonymous.* 3rd ed. New York: Alcoholics Anonymous World Services.

Ameri, A. 1999. "The Effects of Cannabinoids on the Brain." *Progress in Neurobiology* 58, no. 4: 315–48.

American Psychiatric Association. 1987. *Diagnostic and Statistical Manual of Mental Disorders.* 3rd ed. rev. Washington, D.C.: American Psychiatric Association.

———. 1994. *Diagnostic and Statistical Manual of Mental Disorders.* 4th ed. Washington, D.C.: American Psychiatric Association.

Azrin, N. H. 1976. "Improvements in the Community-Reinforcement Approach to Alcoholism." *Behaviour Research and Therapy* 14, no. 5: 339–48.

Beattie, M. 1987. *Co-Dependent No More.* Center City, Minn.: Hazelden Foundation.

Beck, A. T. 1993. "Cognitive Approaches to Stress." In *Principles and Practice of Stress Management,* ed. R. Woolfolk and P. Lehrer. 2nd ed. New York: Guilford Press.

Beck, A. T., F. D. Wright, C. F. Newman, and B. S. Liese. 1991. "Cognitive Therapy of Cocaine Abuse: A Treatment Manual." Unpublished manuscript.

Beck, A. T., F. D. Wright, C. F. Newman, and R. W. Warner. 1993. *Cognitive Therapy of Substance Abuse.* New York: Guilford Press.

Benjamin, A. 1974. *The Helping Interview.* 2nd ed. Boston: Houghton Mifflin.

Bissell, L., and J. E. Royce. 1987. *Ethics for Addiction Professionals.* Center City, Minn.: Hazelden Foundation.

———. 1994. *Ethics for Addiction Professionals.* 2nd ed. Center City, Minn.: Hazelden Information and Education, 1994.

Black, C. 1981. *It Will Never Happen to Me.* Denver: M.A.C. Printing and Publications Division.

Block, R. I., and M. N. Ghoneim. 1993. "Effects of Chronic Marijuana Use on Human Cognition." *Psychopharmacology* 100, nos. 1–2: 219–28.

Bloom, F. E. 1992. "Molecular Genetics and Psychiatry." In *Reflections on Modern Psychiatry,* ed. D. Kupfer. Washington, D.C.: American Psychiatric Press.

Bohman, M. 1978. "Some Genetic Aspects of Alcoholism and Criminality." *Archives of General Psychiatry* 35: 269–76.

Bradshaw, J. 1988. *Healing the Shame That Binds You.* Deerfield Beach, Fla.: Health Communications.

Brady, K. T., and C. L. Randall. 1999. "Gender Differences in Substance Use Disorders." *Psychiatric Clinics of North America* 22: 241–52.

Brook, J. S., E. B. Balka, and M. Whiteman. 1999. "The Risks for Late Adolescence of Early Adolescent Marijuana Use." *American Journal of Public Health* 89, no. 10: 1549–54.

Brook, J. S., et al. 2001. "The Effect of Early Marijuana Use on Later Anxiety and Depressive Symptoms." *NYS Psychologist* (January): 35–39.

Carey, K. B., and C. J. Correia. 1998. "Severe Mental Illness and Addictions: Assessment Considerations." *Addictive Behaviors* 23, no. 6: 735–48.

Carey, K. B., and S. A. Maisto. 1985. "A Review of the Use of Self-Control Techniques in the Treatment of Alcohol Abuse." *Cognitive Therapy and Research* 9: 235–51.

Carkhuff, R. R. 1987. *The Art of Helping VI.* Amherst, Mass.: Human Resource Development Press.

Carroll, K. M. 1998. *A Cognitive-Behavioral Approach: Treating Cocaine Addiction.* National Institute on Drug Abuse, Therapy Manuals for Drug Addiction, Manual 1, U.S. Department of Health and Human Services, National Institutes of Health. Available online at www.nida.nih.gov/TXManuals/CBT1.html.

Cermak, T. L. 1986. *Diagnosing and Treating Co-Dependence.* Minneapolis: Johnson Institute Books.

———. 1989. *Diagnosing and Treating Co-Dependence: A Guide for Professionals Who Work with Chemical Dependents, Their Spouses, and Children.* Minneapolis: Johnson Institute.

Crits-Christoph, P., L. Siqueland, J. Blaine, et al. 1999. "Psychosocial Treatments for Cocaine Dependence: National Institute on Drug Abuse Collaborative Cocaine Treatment Study." *Archives of General Psychiatry* 56: 493–502.

Daley, D. C., and D. E. Mercer. 2002. *Drug Counseling for Cocaine Addiction: The Collaborative Cocaine Treatment Study Model.* National Institute on Drug Abuse, Therapy Manuals for Drug Addiction, Manual 4, U.S. Department of Health and Human Services, National Institutes of Health. Available online at www.nida.nih.gov/TXManuals/DCCA/DCCA1.html.

Daley, D. C., and H. B. Moss. 2002. *Dual Disorders: Counseling Clients with Chemical Dependency and Mental Illness.* 3rd ed. Center City, Minn.: Hazelden.

Daley, D. C., H. Moss, and F. Campbell. 1987. *Dual Disorders.* Center City, Minn.: Hazelden Foundation.

Delos Reyes, C. 2002. "Topics from the Ruth Fox Course for Addiction Medicine." 22nd Annual Ruth Fox Course for Physicians. Program and Abstracts of the American Society of Addiction Medicine 33rd Annual Meeting and Medical-Scientific Conference, Atlanta: April 25–28.

DiClemente, C. C., and J. O. Prochaska. 1985. "Processes and Stages of Change: Coping and Competence in Smoking Behavior Change." In *Coping and Substance Abuse,* ed. S. Shiffman and T. A. Wills, 319–42. New York: Academic Press.

———. 1998. "Toward a Comprehensive Trans-Theoretical Model of Change: Stages of Change and Addictive Behaviors." In *Treating Addictive Behaviors,* ed. W. R. Miller and N. Heather, 3–24. 2nd ed. New York: Plenum Press.

Doyle Pita, D. 1992. *Addictions Counseling.* New York: Crossroad.

———. 1993. *The Dumbo Dilemma.* New York: Crossroad.

Doyle Pita, D., and S. Spaniol, eds. 2002. *A Comprehensive Guide for Integrated Treatment of People with Co-Occurring Disorders.* Boston: Boston University Center for Psychiatric Rehabilitation.

Ellis, A. 1962. *Reason and Emotion in Psychotherapy.* Secaucus, N.J.: Citadel Press.

———. 1972. *Psychotherapy and the Value of a Human Being.* New York: Institute for Rational-Emotive Therapy.

———. 1975. *How to Live with a Neurotic: At Home and at Work.* Rev. ed. New York: Crown.

———. 1977a. "Fun as Psychotherapy." *Rational Living* 12, no. 1: 2–6.

———, Speaker. 1977b. *A Garland of Rational Humorous Songs.* Cassette recording. New York: Institute for Rational Living.

Ellis, A., J. McInerney, R. DiGiuseppe, and R. Yeager. 1988. *Rational Emotive Therapy with Alcoholics and Substance Abusers.* New York: Pergamon Press.

Engel, B. 1990. *The Emotionally Abused Woman.* New York: Ballantine Books.

Erikson, E. H. 1968. *Childhood and Society.* New York: W. W. Norton.

———. 1982. *The Life Cycle Completed.* New York: W. W. Norton.

Fenton, W. S., C. R. Blyler, and R. K. Heinssen. 1997. "Determinants of Medication Compliance in Schizophrenia: Empirical and Clinical Findings." *Schizophrenia Bulletin* 23, no. 4: 637–51.

Fletcher, J. M., J. B. Page, D. J. Francis, K. Copeland, M. J. Naus, C. M. Davis, R. Morris, D. Krauskopf, and P. Santz. 1996. "Cognitive Correlates of Chronic Cannabis Use in Costa Rican Men." *Archives of General Psychiatry* 53: 1051–57.

Freud, S. 1943. *A General Introduction to Psychoanalysis.* New York: Doubleday.

Gilman, A. G., T. W. Rall, A. S. Nies, and P. Taylor, eds. 1998. Goodman and Gilman's *The Pharmacological Basis of Therapeutics,* 8th ed. New York: Pergamon Press.

Glasser, W. 1965. *Reality Therapy: A New Approach to Psychiatry.* New York: Harper & Row.

———. 1976. *Positive Addiction.* New York: Harper & Row.

Gonsiorek, J. 1987. "Treatment of the Therapist." In *Psychotherapists' Sexual Involvement with Clients: Intervention and Prevention,* ed. G. Schoener, J. Milgrom, J. Gonsiorek, E. Luepker, and R. Conroe. Minneapolis: Walk-in Counseling Center.

Goodwin, D. W. 1976. *Is Alcoholism Hereditary?* New York: Oxford University Press.

Gorski, T. T. 1989. "The CENAPS Model of Relapse Prevention Planning." *Journal of Chemical Dependence Treatment* 2: 153–69.

———. 2000. "The CENAPS Model of Relapse Prevention Therapy (CMRPT)." In *Approaches to Drug Abuse Counseling.* Rockville, Md.: NIDA.

Gorski, T., and M. Miller. 1982. *Learning to Live Again: Guidelines for Recovery.* Independence, Mo.: Herald House.

———. *Counselor's Manual for Relapse Prevention with Chemically Dependent Criminal Offenders.* 1996. Rockville, Md.: SAMHSA.

Graham, A. W., T. K. Schultz, and B. B. Wilford, eds. 1998. *Principles of Addiction Medicine.* 2nd ed. Chevy Chase, Md.: American Society of Addiction Medicine.

Green, B. E., and C. Ritter. 2000. "Marijuana Use and Depression." *Journal of Health and Social Behavior* 41, no. 1: 40–49.

Hansen, J. C., R. R. Stevic, and R. W. Warner. 1977. *Counseling.* Boston: Allyn and Bacon.

Heinz, A., P. Ragan, D. W. Jones, D. Hommer, W. Williams, M. B. Knable, J. G. Gorey, L. Doty, C. Geyer, K. S. Lee, R. Coppola, D. R. Weinberger, and M. Linnoila. 1998. "Reduced Central Serotonin Transporters in Alcoholism." *American Journal of Psychiatry* 155: 1544–49.

Heishman, S. J., K. Arasteh, and M. L. Stitzer. 1997. "Comparative Effects of Alcohol and Marijuana on Mood, Memory, and Performance." *Pharmacology, Biochemistry, and Behavior* 58: 97–101.

Hester, R. K., and W. R. Miller, eds. 1989. *Handbook of Alcoholism Treatment Approaches*. New York: Pergamon Press.

Higgens, S. T., A. J. Budney, W. K. Bickel, F. E. Foerg, R. Donham, and G. J. Badger. 1994. "Incentives Improve Outcome in Outpatient Behavioral Treatment of Cocaine Dependence." *Archives of General Psychiatry* 51, no. 7: 568–76.

Howell, E. F. 2002. "Addiction and Special Issues." American Society of Addiction Medicine 33rd Annual Meeting and Medical-Scientific Conference, April 25–28, Atlanta.

Jehu, D., J. Davis, T. Garrett, L. M. Jorenson, and G. R. Schoener. 1995. *Patients as Victims: Sexual Abuse in Psychotherapy and Counseling*. New York: John Wiley.

Jellinek, E. M. 1960. *The Disease Concept of Alcoholism*. New Haven, Conn.: Hill House Press.

———. 1962. "Phases of Alcohol Addiction." In *Society, Culture, and Drinking Patterns*, ed. D. J. Pittman and S. R. Snyder. New York: John Wiley.

Jones, R. T., et al. 1981. "Clinical Relevance of Cannabis Tolerance and Dependence." *Journal of Clinical Pharmacology* 21, nos. 8–9 Suppl.: 143S–152S.

Kinney, J., and G. Leaton. 1983. *Loosening the Grip*. St. Louis, Mo.: C. V. Mosby.

———. 2003. *Loosening the Grip: A Handbook of Alcohol Information*. 7th ed. Boston: McGraw-Hill.

Koob, G. F. 2002. "Drug Addiction, Reward Dysregulation, and Allostasis Addiction." 22nd Annual Ruth Fox Course for Physicians. Program and Abstracts of the American Society of Addiction Medicine 33rd Annual Meeting and Medical-Scientific Conference, April 25–28, Atlanta.

Kübler-Ross, E. 1969. *On Death and Dying*. New York: Macmillan.

Leshner, A. I. 2000. "Treating the Brain in Drug Abuse." *NIDA Notes* 15, no. 4.

Liddle, H. A., et al. 2001. "Multidimensional Family Therapy for Adolescent Drug Abuse: Results of a Randomized Clinical Trial." *American Journal of Drug and Alcohol Abuse* 27, no. 4: 651–87.

Liese, B. S., and A. T. Beck. 1997. "Back to Basics: Fundamental Therapy Skills for Keeping Drug-Dependent Individuals in Treatment." *NIDA Research Monograph*, no. 165.

Linehan, M. M. 1993a. *Cognitive-Behavioral Treatment of Borderline Personality Disorder*. New York: Pergamon Press.

———. *Skill Training Manual for Treating Borderline Personality Disorder*. 1993b. New York: Guilford Press.

Mackay, P. W., D. M. Donovan, and G. A. Marlatt. 1991. "Cognitive and Behavioral Approaches to Alcohol Abuse." In *Clinical Textbook of Addictive Disorders*, ed. R. J. Frances and S. I. Miller, 452–81. New York: Guilford Press.

Marlatt, G. A. 1983. "The Controlled Drinking Controversy: A Commentary." *American Psychologist* 10: 1097–1110.

Marlatt, G. A., and J. R. Gordon, eds. 1985. *Relapse Prevention: Maintenance Strategies in the Treatment of Addictive Behaviors.* New York: Guilford Press.

Maslow, A. 1970. *Motivation and Personality,* 2nd ed. New York: Harper & Row.

Maultsby, M. C. 1978. *The Rational Behavioral Alcoholic-Relapse Prevention Treatment Method.* Lexington, Ky.: Rational Self-Help Aids.

Mercer, D. E., and G. E. Woody. 1999. *An Individual Drug Counseling Approach to Treat Cocaine Addiction: The Collaborative Cocaine Treatment Study Model.* National Institute on Drug Abuse, Therapy Manuals for Drug Addiction, Manual 3, U.S. Department of Health and Human Services, National Institutes of Health. Available online at www.nida.nih.gov/ TXManuals/IDCA/IDCA1.html.

Meyers, R. J., and J. E. Smith. 1995. *Clinical Guide to Alcohol Treatment: The Community Reinforcement Approach.* New York: Guilford Press.

Miller, P. M. 1976. "A Comprehensive Behavioral Approach to the Treatment of Alcoholism." In *Alcoholism: Interdisciplinary Approaches to an Enduring Problem*, ed. Ralph Tarter and A. Arthur Sugerman. Reading, Mass.: Addison-Wesley.

Miller, W. R., ed. 1999. "Enhancing Motivation for Change in Substance Abuse Treatment." In *Treatment Improvement Protocol* (TIP) Series No. 35. Rockville, Md.: Center for Substance Abuse Treatment.

Miller, W. R., R. G. Benefield, and J. S. Tonigan. 1993. "Enhancing Motivation for Change in Problem Drinking: A Controlled Comparison of Two Therapist Styles." *Journal of Consulting and Clinical Psychology* 6, no. 13: 455–61.

Miller, W. R., and S. Rollnick. 1991. *Motivational Interviewing: Preparing People to Change Addictive Behavior.* New York: Guilford Press.

———. 2002. *Motivational Interviewing: Preparing People for Change.* 2nd ed. New York: Guilford Press.

Miller, W. R., A. Zweben, C. C. DiClemente, and R. Rychtarik. 1992. *Motivational Enhancement Therapy Manual: A Clinical Research Guide for Therapists Treating Individuals with Alcohol Abuse and Dependence.* Project MATCH Monograph Series, vol. 2. Rockville, Md.: National Institute on Alcohol Abuse and Alcoholism.

Mueser, K. T., R. E. Drake, and D. L. Noordsy. 1998. "Integrated Mental Health and Substance Abuse Treatment for Severe Psychiatric Disorders." *Journal of Practical Psychiatry and Behavioral Health* 4: 129–39.

Mueser, K. T., and L. Fox. 1998. *Stagewise Family Treatment for Dual Disorders Treatment Manual.* Dartmouth, N.H.: NH-Dartmouth Psychiatric Research Center.

NIDA (National Institute on Drug Abuse). 2000. "Treatment Methods for Women." Infofax.

———. 2002. "High School and Youth Trends." Infofax.

National Household Survey on Drug Abuse. 2002. Substance Abuse and Mental Health Services Administration, Office of Applied Studies.

Nowinski, J., S. Baker, and K. Carroll. 1994. *Twelve-Step Facilitation Therapy Manual: A Clinical Research Guide for Therapists Treating Individuals with Alcohol Abuse and Dependence.* National Institute on Alcohol Abuse and Alcoholism, Project MATCH Monograph series, vol. 1. NIH Publication No. 94-3722, Washington, D.C.: Superintendent of Documents, U.S. Government Printing Office.

Osher, F. C., and L. L. Kofoed. 1989. "Treatment of Patients with Psychiatric and Psychoactive Substance Abuse Disorders." *Hospital Community Psychiatry* 40: 1025–30.

Patrick, G., and F. A. Struve. 2000. "Reduction of Auditory P50 Gating Response in Marijuana Users: Further Supporting Data." *Clinical Electroencephalography* 31, no. 2: 88–93.

Perkinson, R. R., and A. E. Jongsma. 2001. *The Addictions Treatment Planner.* 2nd ed. New York: John Wiley & Sons.

Pope, K. S., and J. Bouhoutsos. 1986. *Sexual Intimacy between Therapists and Patients.* New York: Praeger.

Rippere, V., and R. Williams, eds. 1985. *Wounded Healers: Mental Health Workers' Experiences of Depression.* New York: John Wiley.

Rogers, C. R. 1951. *Client-Centered Therapy.* Boston: Houghton Mifflin.

———. 1961. *On Becoming a Person.* Boston: Houghton Mifflin.

Rosenberg, S. D., R. E. Drake, G. L. Wolford, K. T. Mueser, T. E. Oxman, R. M. Vidaver, K. L. Carrieri, and R. Luckoor. 1998. "The Dartmouth Assessment of Lifestyle Instrument (Dali): A Substance Abuse Disorder Screen for People with Severe Mental Illness." *American Journal of Psychiatry* 155: 232–38.

Roth, M. D., A. Arora, S. H. Barsky, E. C. Kleerup, M. Simmons, and D. P. Tashkin. 1998. "Airway Inflammation in Young Marijuana and Tobacco Smokers." *American Journal of Respiratory and Critical Care Medicine* 157: 928–37.

Rustin, T. A. 2002. "Nicotine and Nicotine Dependence." 22nd Annual Ruth Fox Course for Physicians. Program and Abstracts of the American Society of Addiction Medicine 33rd Annual Meeting and Medical-Scientific Conference, April 25–28, Atlanta.

Sarafian, T. A., J. A. Magallanes, H. Shau, D. Tashkin, and M. D. Roth. 1999. "Oxidative Stress Produced by Marijuana Smoke: An Adverse Effect Enhanced by Cannabinoids." *American Journal of Respiratory Cell and Molecular Biology* 20, no. 6: 1286–93.

Schoener, G. 1987. "Assessment and Development of Rehabilitation Plans for the Therapist." In *Psychotherapists' Sexual Involvement with Clients: Intervention and Prevention,* ed. G. Schoener, J. Milgrom, G. Gonsiorek, E. Luepker, and R. Conroe. Minneapolis: Walk-in Counseling Center.

Simpson, D. D., G. W. Joe, G. A. Rowan-Szal, and J. M. Greener. 1997. "Drug Abuse Treatment Process Components That Improve Retention." *Journal of Substance Abuse Treatment* 14, no. 6: 565–72.

Snow, Candace, and David Willard, R.N. 1990. *I'm Dying to Take Care of You: Nurses and Codependence; Breaking the Cycles.* Redmond, Wash.: Professional Counselor Books.

Srivastava, M. D., B. I. Srivastava, and B. Brouhard. 1998. "Delta-9 Tetrahydrocannabinol and Cannabidiol Alter Cytokine Production by Human Immune Cells." *Immunopharmacology* 40, no. 3: 179–85.

Tashkin, D. P. 1990. "Pulmonary Complications of Smoked Substance Abuse." *Western Journal of Medicine* 152: 525–30.

Trimpey, Jack. 1990. "Rational Recovery: A Bold New Approach to Addiction Care." *The Humanist* (January–February).

Truax, C., and R. Carkhuff. 1967. *Toward Effective Counseling and Psychotherapy.* Chicago: Aldine Publishing Co.

U.S. Substance Abuse and Mental Health Services Administration, Office of Applied Studies. Summary of Findings from the 2000 National Household Survey on Drug Abuse. Rockville, Md.

White, K. 1989. *Intimacy Scoring Manual.* Social Science Document Service.

White, W. 2001. *Critical Incidents: Ethical Issues in the Prevention and Treatment of Addiction.* 2nd ed. Bloomington, Ill.: Chestnut Health Systems.

Wilson, W., R. Mathew, T. Turkington, T. Hawk, R. E. Coleman, and J. Provenzale. 2000. "Brain Morphological Changes and Early Marijuana Use: A Magnetic Resonance and Positron Emission Tomography Study." *Journal of Addictive Diseases* 19, no. 1: 1–22.

Yalom, L. D. 1985. *The Theory and Practice of Group Psychotherapy.* 3rd ed. New York: Basic Books, 1985.

Zhang, Z.-F., H. Morgenstern, M. R. Spitz, D. P. Tashkin, G.-P. Yu, J. R. Marshall, T. C. Hsu, and P. S. Stimson. 1999. "Marijuana Use and Increased Risk of Squamous Cell Carcinoma of the Head and Neck." *Cancer Epidemiology, Biomarkers and Prevention* 6: 1071–78.

Zhu, L. X., M. Stolina, S. Sharma, B. Gardner, M. D. Roth, D. P. Tashkin, and S. M. Dubinett. 2000. "Delta-9 Tetrahydrocannabinol Inhibits Antitumor Immunity by a CB-2 Receptor-Mediated, Cytokine Dependent-Pathway." *Journal of Immunology* 165 no. 1: 373–80.

ABOUT THE AUTHOR

Currently Dr. Doyle-Pita, a licensed psychologist, is a lecturer and clinical supervisor at the University of Massachusetts, Boston, where she has taught courses in addictions counseling for seventeen years. She also works as an adjunct professor at Boston University.

Her clinical specialties include addictions, dual disorders, and the psychosocial treatment of mental illness. Dr. Doyle-Pita also has worked in several outpatient settings. These include detox treatment centers, court-mandated addictions treatment, residential addiction treatment for health professionals, and outpatient settings for mental health and substance abuse. She also maintains her own private practice in the Boston area.

Ms. Doyle-Pita holds a B.A. in Psychology from the University of Massachusetts, Boston; an M.A. in Clinical Psychology from Loyola College; and the Ph.D. in Personality Psychology from Boston University. Dr. Doyle-Pita is a certified Rational Emotive Therapist.

Dr. Doyle-Pita has been publishing articles in the area of addictions since 1986. She is also the author of *The Dumbo Dilemma: Learning to Fly in Spite of Life's Worries* (Crossroad, 1993) and co-editor of *Integration of Dual Diagnosis Theory, Research, and Treatment* (IAPSRS, 2002).

Dianne lives in Boxborough, Massachusetts, with her family.